BOURNE
and BRED

A Dunstable boyhood
between the wars

Colin Bourne

First published June 1990
by
The Book Castle
12 Church Street
Dunstable
Bedfordshire LU5 4RU

ISBN 1 871199 40 9

Cover design by Trevor Wood, incorporating the
chocolate and blue colours of Dunstable
Grammar School.

Photographs
Front cover – High Street North, the old Town Hall.
  – 'Under 14' XI cricket.

Back cover – Floods in Dunstable, May 1936. The
  spire of the Methodist Church, The
  Square, in the background.

  – Country scene. Old-fashioned corn
  stooks in a field on the edge of Dunstable.

  – Aerial view of the Grammar School and
  its surrounds.

Printed and bound by:
Antony Rowe Ltd., Chippenham

CONTENTS

To my mother and father
who gave so much
and
to all those Dunstable folk
who weaved a rich tapestry of life

ACKNOWLEDGMENTS

I would like to thank those people who, in one way or another, have helped towards the publication of this book. Particularly I would like to mention my wife, Joy, for deciphering some fairly undistinguishable writing, together with a host of instructions, in undertaking the typing, and to Eric Baldock and Fred Moore for their support, observations and gentle words of wisdom in the early days of its preparation.

These thanks also include those who have lent photographs, booklets and documents which, apart from being of assistance, have given me many interesting hours of contemplation.

Many of the photographs are from my own family albums, but others are credited at the end of the book.

'Our life is a dream,
Our time as a stream
Glides swiftly away,
And the fugitive moment refuses to stay'

Dunstable north-west quadrant, 1935 Official Guide

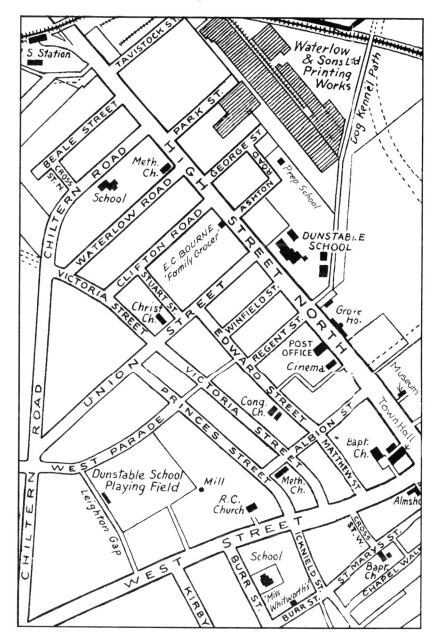

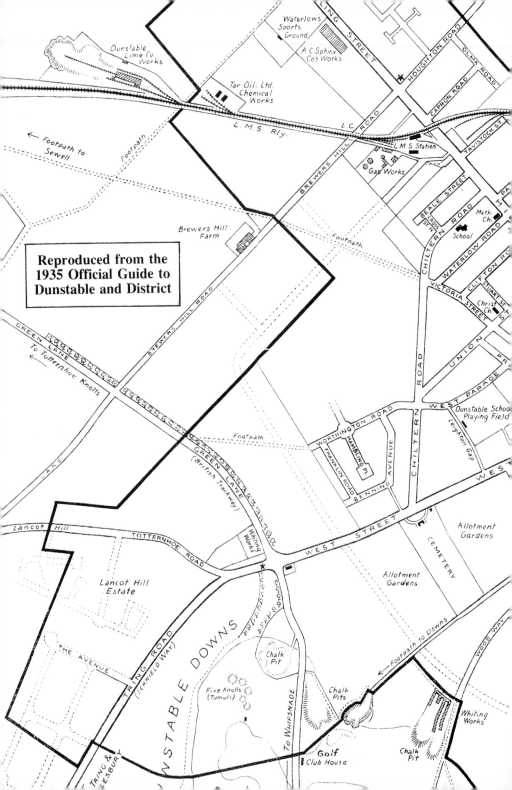

Reproduced from the
1935 Official Guide to
Dunstable and District

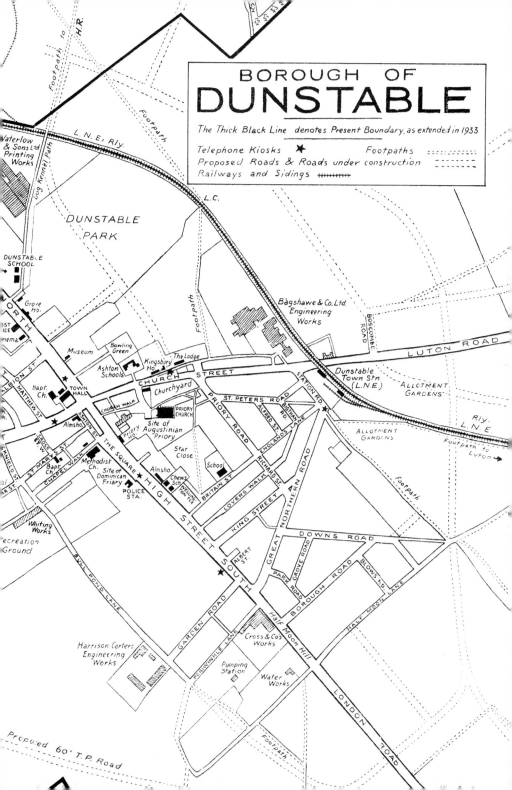

BOROUGH OF
DUNSTABLE

The Thick Black Line denotes Present Boundary, as extended in 1933

Telephone Kiosks   ✹   Footpaths   ·············
Proposed Roads & Roads under construction   - - - - - -
Railways and Sidings   ++++++++

Footpath to H.R.

Waterlow & Sons Ltd. Printing Works

L. N. E. Rly.

Dog Kennel Path

Footpath

DUNSTABLE PARK

DUNSTABLE SCHOOL

NORTH

Grove Ho.

POST OFFICE

Cinema

Museum

Bowling Green

Ashton Schools

Kingsbury Ho.

The Lodge

L.C.

Bagshawe & Co. Ltd. Engineering Works

BOSCOMBE ROAD

LUTON ROAD

CHURCH STREET

ALBION ST.

MATTHEW ST.

Bapt. Ch.

TOWN HALL

CHURCH WALK

Almsho.

Churchyard

PRIORY CHURCH

Priory Ho.

Site of Augustinian Priory

ST. PETERS ROAD

PRIORY ROAD

ALFRED RD.

BETHANY RD.

STATION RD.

Dunstable Town Stn. (L.N.E.)

ALLOTMENT GARDENS

ALLOTMENT GARDENS

Rly. L. N. E.

Footpath to Luton

CROSS ST.

ST. MARYS ST.

CHAPEL WALK

Bapt. Chapel

Methodist Ch.

Site of Dominican Friary

THE SQUARE

Almsho.

Chews School

WINDS FORGE ST.

Star Close

School

ENGLANDS ROAD

BRITAIN ST.

RICHARD ST.

POLICE STA.

HIGH STREET SOUTH

LOVERS WALK

KING STREET

GREAT NORTHERN ROAD

PARK ROAD

GROVE ROAD

BOROUGH ROAD

DOWNS ROAD

BLOWS RD LANE

HALF MOON LANE

Whiting Works

Recreation Ground

BULL POND LANE

ALBERT ST.

GARDEN ROAD

PERIWINKLE LANE

Harrison Carters Engineering Works

Cross & Co. Works

Pumping Station

Water Works

HALF MOON HILL

LONDON ROAD

Footpath

Proposed 60' T.P. Road

Chapter 1

THE SHOP – and the Grocer

It was quite an ordinary shop, really. It was not one that you would go out of your way to see or necessarily stop and look at for more than a moment if you were passing for the first time. But it had a certain quality, a certain homeliness, a certain feeling of warmth about it, which was due very much to the care given to it by the grocer who owned the shop.

As you looked at it, standing on the pavement of High Street North those fifty or sixty odd years ago, it had a small window on the left hand side, then there was the entrance, then on the right came the large window. Over the top, neatly sign-written, was the grocer's name and an indication that it was a grocery and provisions shop.

The windows were referred to by the grocer, simply, as the small and big windows. The small window would be changed once a month, the big one every fortnight and that would be done on an evening, when the grocer had shut up shop, or maybe on a Thursday afternoon, early closing day, if it was wet. The windows offered displays of the shop's contents. Tins of produce would be neatly stacked into pyramids, and packets of this and that would be carefully arranged to give an attractive overall picture. At the back of the big window was a draped half-curtain and clear, clean notices in the grocer's own printing would be hung where appropriate. There was nothing frantic about the display, nor were there two or three items surrounded by clever objects that had nothing to do with groceries. It was not that kind of shop.

The narrow entrance, with its door set back a few feet, had just enough room to put three or four small sacks of corn, seed and dog biscuits on the step and still leave room for the customers. The door was the old-fashioned sort of door, with a solid piece at the bottom, where there was a horizontal letter box, then the main plate of glass, the corners of which had glazed advertisements for Oxo and Ty-Phoo tea, followed by a skylight type panel at the top. In the good weather it stood

1

open. But in poor weather it was closed and as it was opened it clanged, where a little lever at the top rang a bell. When the grocer closed the shop, at lunch time and in the evening, he pulled down a roller blind over the main glass and attached it to a hook. If the hook was missed the blind shot up again at great speed, much to the delight of the grocer's small boy.

Inside the shop itself, around where the customers stood on the wooden floor (or sat, if they were rather frail, on one rather old, spindly legged chair with a hard seat which had a pattern of small holes in it) there were two counters.

The one on the left was the provision counter, the one on the right the grocery counter. Joining the latter at the far end and across the shop were display shelves. Here the grocer displayed dummy cartons and tins, confectioneries such as Bakewell Tarts and Lyons Swiss Rolls and a few flat boxes of apples and oranges. These shelves really came to life at Christmas, when boxes of colourful crackers were the backdrop to all sorts of goodies. Turkish Delight (in round wooden drums) vied with Tunisian dates, Meltis orange and lemon slices, Batgers Chinese Figs, special tins of biscuits, handsomely painted tea caddies and bottles of non-alcoholic ginger, raisin and orange wine from Beaufoys.

The provision counter was where all the fats were served out. It was also where the bacon was sliced, exactly to the thickness required, on one of those lovely old red and white slicing machines. Ham, for the grocer was known for his home-baked ham and tongue, was cut also. Lard and cheese were cut separately and placed on a square of provision paper on the immaculately clean weighing machine and again the customer had exactly what was wanted. The grocer was an honest, good man and he never, ever served his customers short or knowingly sold them inferior goods. Because of this and the fact that he always had a cheerful greeting and a great sense of humour, his customers liked coming into his shop and he was very much part of the community. A kindly man, he served the needs of those around him and was often asked for advice and help, which was always freely given. He had time for his customers, there was no great impersonal hurry and rush. He realised that for many it was a social occasion to come to the shop. The travellers of the various firms also liked visiting the shop and over the years a friendly and trusting acquaintance grew with them.

The main cheese for the provision counter was initially cut outside the back of the shop with a cheese wire, slicing through the great round drum of cheese, an action that needed a lot of strength and no little care. Segments were then set out further down the counter, along with other small round boxes of St. Ivel pre-packed cheeses and wickerwork baskets of eggs.

Golden Acre butter, Blue Band margarine, Atora suet were stored in the large shelves ranging along the shop behind the counter, which for some peculiar reason, probably because there was advertising on it, were divided at one point by a full length mirror. These shelves were stacked also with tins of Heinz and Crosse & Blackwell soups (mulligatawny and ox-tail were the favourites) Heinz baked beans, jars of chutney and piccalilli and pickled onions, H.P. and O.K. sauce, Daddies sauce, tomato ketchup, Fray Bentos squat tins of corned beef, Libby's peaches and apricots, Bartlett pears, Epicure pineapple, Chivers' fruit salad, somebody's black cherries.

Here as well were the tins of fish – red salmon, pilchards and sardines with those little keys that, hopefully, rolled back and opened the tin. Glacé cherries from a jar were spooned out and weighed. Seniors and Shippams pastes of all sorts of concoctions in little glass jars were squeezed in with Ideal milk, Tate & Lyle's golden syrup ('Out of the strong came forth sweetness') and Fowler's Black West India treacle. Cubes of Oxo, Bisto (with the Bisto Kids to the fore), Sage & Onion lay alongside bottles of Bovril, with the picture of a man in striped pyjamas sitting on top of an imaginary Bovril bottle.

At the back of the shop on this side, hidden from sight as though they were not really the sort of things to put on show, were the packets of dog biscuits – Spillers Shapes, Spratts, Melox Marvels – and cat food, firelighters and odd assorted items that a customer had asked for, the grocer had obtained and then had not sold all of them. Here too were drawers of prunes and dried apricots, lentils and dried peas.

The grocery counter, opposite, was where the main serving was done, the items collected together, the money taken and the delivery orders made up in the evenings for the errand boy to take out on the shop's bicycle, with its big basket on the front and a smaller one on the back. These orders had come over the black upright single stand telephone in the house and the errand boy went out weekly to the far flung corners of Dunstable – to West Street and Tring Road, to Downs Road and Great Northern Road, to Garden Road and the top of High Street South, along Church Street and down past the Chalk Cutting. Those were the days when a steady set of customers, valuable indeed, ordered their groceries over the 'phone and expected their orders to be duly delivered. And if one item was wrong, or an item had been missed, back the errand boy had to go and journey forth again.

At the back of the grocery counter, lining the wall, again there were wooden shelves, high ones and low ones. Here were the cereals of the day – packets of Force ('Lucky Jim'), Shredded Wheat, Quaker Oats and Scott's Porridge Oats with the picture of the Scotsman in his kilt swinging his hammer. No such things as Rice Krispies, these were not yet born. The flour was stacked here, taking up lots of room – McDougall's Plain and Self-Raising, Thorne's Self-Raising, Lilley's

3

Plain, followed by all the types of sugar (Tate & Lyle, of course) and the packets of tea – Ty-Phoo, Brooke Bond, Mazawattee, Lyons, Priory, several with their colourful labels depicting the picking of leaves in some far away clime. Small cartons of Borwick's Baking Powder found their place near the flour, too.

There was a small shelf of cigarettes and sweets, not many, enough to serve those who wanted them. Ardath, Park Drive, Kensitas, Woodbines, Craven 'A', Players, de Reszke. Ship matches, Bryant & May, Blue Cross. Mars bars, Milky Way, Nestlé's chocolate, Cadbury's twopenny bars of milk or fruit and nut chocolate. Nearby jostled tins of Ovaltine, Horlicks, Bourn-Vita, Cadbury's Drinking Chocolate in its purple tin, Nestlé's, Fry's cocoa and bottles of Camp coffee. Alongside were the soft and fizzy drinks – Robinson's Pearl Barley water, Kia-Ora lemon and orange squash, Rose's lime juice, Idris lemonade and cherryade, Icefoam, Eiffel Tower, Green's (of Brighton) lemonade crystals and one or two Burgess' soda water syphons.

Another small shelf held the green and white tins of Andrew's Liver Salts, mingling with small oval tins of smarmy green Brilliantine, nightlights and the tooth pastes – Gibbs Dentifrice (those Fairy Castles of long ago), Macleans, Euthymol and the yellow packets of Kolynos.

Then there were the sweet things beloved at children's parties and by a good many grown-ups too. Chivers' and Rowntree's jellies, Pearce Duff's blancmanges, Symington's table creams. Jars and jars of jam stood close by, along with Bird's custard and Brown & Polson cornflour. Hartley's Raspberry jam was the best seller, so the grocer always made sure he had a good stock in of this, but there was also Chivers' and Robertson's jams (ah, that much-loved and happy golliwog) and Chivers' Old English marmalade, together with lemon curd, honey (Bedfordshire honey) and Marmite.

Add Colman's mustard, Saxa and Cerebos salt, cayenne pepper, red packets of Sun-Maid raisins and made up bags of currants and sultanas and the grocery shelves were a veritable haven of rejoicing.

All these could be seen, along with the coffee grinder fixed to the counter from which came the most delicious aroma when the handle was turned to grind the coffee beans. But under the counter and on the lower shelves, largely unseen, were the cleaning materials. Robin Starch, Dolly bags, Reckitt's blue bags (good for wasp stings), large bars of Lifebuoy and Sunlight soap, Wright's coaltar and the more delicately perfumed Lux Toilet and Palm-Olive. Zebo grate polish, Brasso, Silvo, Mansion polish, Ronuk, Cherry Blossom, Kiwi, Meltonian and Nuggett's shoe polish, Dales' dubbin, Omo, Persil, Lux flakes, Rinso, soda made up in 2lb bags of dark blue cartridge paper, Harpic, sticks of candles, and, from the whiting works at the corner of Victoria Street and Chiltern Road, five minutes walk away, blocks of whiting wrapped in old newspapers (mostly The News Chronicle).

The whole shop and all its wooden furniture was kept clean and free from bits and pieces by the diligence of the grocer, who had set a high standard and kept to it. It was not a poky shop, but it was not a large one by any means; it just made use of the space to the best advantage, lit in the winter by old type electric lights that hung down on chains from a rather old wooden ceiling.

But there were three other things that added character to that shop. One was the biscuit rack immediately at the back of the big window, behind the curtain. This was a long, hinged stand where eight lots of glass containers, much the same size as one of those big, square biscuit tins, swung free, showing their delectable contents. It had been given by one of the biscuit firms, the name of the firm was over the top, but it was used for all kinds, to supplement the tins themselves that often stood on the floor nearby.

Here were the famous names. Here were the big five, each of them having a speciality amongst their biscuits. So the customer asked for Crawford's Shortbread, Jacob's Cream Crackers, Peek Frean's Assorted, Huntley & Palmer's Bourbon, McVitie & Price's Digestive. Each of them had an extra plus mark in their marks of quality, each of them were loved in their own turn. And some of their Christmas catalogues needed to be drooled over – thick, shiny paper, with an exciting fragrance, you would almost smell the biscuits on the pages.

The second character item was two rows of small drawers, about 6″ in depth, each with a centre knob, that divided the whole length of the top and bottom shelves behind the grocery counter. There must have been about thirty, give or take, and here the grocer had stored all sorts of things, including some of his working material. But for the customer, spices and medicine, flavourings and pills. Odd items, wanted at some time, perhaps only once a year by one customer. Many of them had to be weighed.

Thus there were nutmegs, ginger, cloves, angelica (which came in long sticks and had to be cut up), cinnamon, mixed herbs, peppercorns, Carter's Little Liver Pills, Beecham Powders, essence of vanilla, digestive pills, twists of Aspro (the grocer was often asked for two Aspros and he would twist these off a concertina type strip), eucalyptus sweets, peppermints of diabolical strength, flat, brown cough sweets of an extremely hot nature, fly papers (fly papers? – these were unrolled, hung up in the kitchen or living room and the sticky substance on them attracted the flies, who therefore got stuck; when about thirty were caught the paper was taken down and another one put up.) If you opened the right drawer, every now and again, there came an aroma borne by the big sailing riggers from the blue seas of the spice islands. Magic.

5

The third point centred around a small counter, behind the high, cross display stand, where a lot of preparatory weighing up was done. Below the counter were four very large and very heavy drawers. These drawers were full of demerara sugar, soft light brown sugar, butter beans and haricot beans, all of which were made up in cartons by the grocer, tucked in at the top and weighed on the small pair of scales nearby. These were mysterious, dark drawers and if you wanted to you could put your hand in the beans, hold it up and let them all slip smoothly away through your fingers, a tingling, gratifying experience.

But also on the top of this dimly-lit counter were three old dimly-painted jars of shag. Old men would come in to the shop, mainly of an early morning, and ask the grocer for 'a penn'th of shag, please mister'. The grocer would go to one of the ancient jars, weigh up a pennyworth of shag on a thin piece of paper and pass it over. The customer was served.

This then was the shop that the grocer owned and looked after. The grocer himself was of that era when the customer was always right and he accepted that. He had come to Dunstable from south London, on the borders of Kent, at the end of the First World War with his wife and young daughter, had set up his business and all through that life he worked long hours and he worked hard. He had had very little education, but he was good with figures, he loved the well-written word and he had great faith.

He had the valued support of his wife (who, amongst other attributes made delicious mince pies at Christmas, which were sold in the shop with considerable acclaim) and a happy family. He made only a humble profit by present-day standards, but he managed to give both his daughter and his son, born later, a good education. He was a regular worshipper and member of the Methodist Church and held many offices there, giving of his spare time generously. He loved the countryside, being particularly knowledgeable on butterflies and moths. He and his wife made a beautiful garden behind the shop and house, where it was hard to believe that it was just off the busy Watling Street, with its thundering lorries. He was a keen sportsman, although playing little himself. He was a man of simple taste, kindhearted and understanding. He is still remembered affectionately now, by those who knew him.

His was a shop that is hardly seen these days and he was a type of old-fashioned grocer that has passed from the scene, for which we are all the poorer.

My sister and I remember the shop well and with much pleasure. And we remember the grocer with great affection and love, as, if you are fortunate, children do remember their father, however the years roll on.

Chapter 2

HIGH STREET NORTH

I have deliberately included the description of the shop and the grocer as the first chapter in these recollections because it was the shop and the house and garden behind that was the centre of my life from the time that I was brought back to it as a babe of some four or five days standing (well, lying, actually) a few days before Christmas, 1924, until the early years of the Second World War.

I say 'house' but we never really referred to it as our house. It was our 'home'. If anyone asked where we lived we said that our *home* was at 131 High Street North. That was because, above everything else, it *was* a home and I was very fortunate indeed to have been brought up by loving parents in a home that seemed like a home the moment you stepped through the door. I do not mean that it was untidy by any means – mother would never ever have had that – but not every single item was put away, it was not a museum, you did not have to tread gently and be careful where you had to sit down. There was a happy link between shop and home, family and friends, obedience, civility and warmth. So I remember those early years with great gratitude and thanksgiving.

My birth certificate states that I was born at 86 Great Northern Road. In those days Priory Road and parts of Great Northern Road were 'the' roads of the town. They had big houses, large gardens and were often inhabited by the civic dignitaries and well-off business people of the community. So I suppose it was natural to find a private nursing home tucked away in the vicinity, for that is what number 86 was. I know (at least I was told later, I don't remember it at the time) that a Mrs. Peeke was involved on this auspicious occasion.

She was the nurse, but also the owner and manageress of the home and as she was the first person that I met physically it is worth recording that she was a Miss Atkins before she married a musical Australian and went to live nearby in Priory Road. By a 'musical Australian' I mean, of course, that Mr. Peeke was an Australian who was fond of music, in fact he had a pipe organ in his house. Strangely enough, in all my travels and in meeting thousands of people, I have never personally met anyone else by the name of Peeke, or Peak, or Peake. The only association is the one that goes with Mr. Frean.

My father apparently walked home very late at night or in the early hours of the morning from Great Northern Road to High Street North, having just been to see his wife and look at his new-born son and was accosted by the local policeman in the middle of the town. After all, if you were found walking about Dunstable in those days in the middle of the night, it is likely that you were up to no good. No proper minded and sensible citizen did that. Father waved his arms in the air and exclaimed 'I've got a son, I've got a son!' So the policeman and the grocer solemnly and joyfully at the same time shook hands and the arm of the law waved the law-abiding citizen on his way.

One hundred and thirty-one High Street North was (and still is as far as the number is concerned) more or less half-way between Union Street and Clifton Road, right opposite Ashton Road, a short street which went down the side of the Grammar School grounds, (where the tennis courts were and where the annual town tennis tournament took place, a big event which went on all week, 6d entry for the public on the weekday evenings, one shilling for Finals Day on the Saturday), before disappearing left by the side of Ashton Lodge and meeting George Street opposite a rather nondescript newspaper shop under the name of de Gerdon (rumoured to be a French count) and close to the main gates of Waterlow & Sons, the big printing works.

That part of High Street North in which I grew up and at least for the first twelve years of my life, was very much a character part of Dunstable, an alternating quiet and busy market town according to the time of the day and the day of the week, and which spread out from the cross roads in its centre, where the ancient British Icknield Way crossed the Roman Watling Street. I caught that character just in time, and because of the impressionable days of childhood and early boyhood, can savour it now, conjuring up the scenes and the people that made up my early life. With the advent of the A. C. Sphinx Sparking Plug Company (the A.C. Delco of to-day) into the town in 1934, industry spreading elsewhere, fences, trees and open fields disappearing and the start of the war, the character began to disappear and in many cases the characters themselves went also.

There were distinct areas of Dunstable, of the town itself. The basic layout and the names of the four big main roads, were quite simple for me to understand. One street, High Street South, went south to London (what was London I used to wonder, it sounded like an awfully big place), one – High Street North – went north. Another – West Street – was one mile from the centre of the town to the slope of the Downs and the start of the Green Lanes opposite (more about those anon) and the fourth – Church Street – which had been called East Street in much earlier years, went to Luton. What happened after Luton I really did not know, at least not for some years.

Those people who lived further up High Street South, in the main, did not really know the area in High Street North in which we lived, unless of course they worked in the vicinity or knew the shop. Likewise there were many citizens of High Street North who had very little idea as to what occurred in the southern end of the town beyond Britain Street, for example. West Street and Church Street were different somehow, because Church Street was not all that long compared with the other main thoroughfares and West Street was the street that you could walk up to get to the Downs and the country and was a promenade on Sunday evenings in the summer. Up one side and down the other, with perhaps a little sit down on the sloping face of the Downs or a short excursion into Green Lanes, past the whiting works on the corner.

But there was also the centre of Dunstable, and the centre of the town did not really belong to any of the streets. It was the hub of the universe. It included the tall spire and the large buildings of the Wesleyan Methodist Church, the cattle market on The Square, Middle Row, the Town Hall and its striking (in every sense) clock which could be seen for miles around and to which generations of Dunstablians looked up to see what time it was (of several Philistine acts carried out in Dunstable the pulling down of the Town Hall and the desecration of the clock was just about the worst), the twice weekly market with the line of covered stalls (when not in use stored at the back of the Town Hall yard) and which stretched down from the corner of West Street to Albion Street, the big Baptist Church, the Red Lion Hotel on the corner of Church Street opposite to the Home & Colonial, The Maltings and a whole variety of shops where you could shop for virtually anything. It was a proper centre.

As far as High Street North was concerned, we reckoned that the centre of Dunstable stopped around Albion Street and the Sugar Loaf Hotel. So we did not count, as part of *our* road, Freddie Monk's draper's emporium, Eddie Hunt's confectionery shop (to which I was sometimes sent, on behalf of my father for packets of cigarettes), World Stores (groceries) with its big nameplate in gold letters behind blue glass, Gibbards Corn Stores, the up-market Confectionery Bazaar of the Misses Omer and Harlow, Charlie Cole's cycle shop with its old-fashioned 'Ordinary' bicycle up high, Charlie Allcorn, Estate Agent and Auctioneer (one of only two Estate Agent's 'shops' in the High Street and with a window that was always chock-block full of large, printed posters), the little Dunstable Museum tucked away at the back of Cycles & Wireless, the Enterprise Printing Works, also tucked away, the

Telephone : Dunstable 41.   Telegrams : "Allcorn, Dunstable."

Chas. A. Allcorn, F.A.I.

Auctioneer, Valuer,

Estate and Transfer Agent.

Sale of Stock in Dunstable Market every Wednesday,
at 2 o'clock.

" The Auction and Estate Offices."

HIGH STREET, DUNSTABLE.

Advertisement for Mr. Allcorn's business in High Street North, opposite the Town Hall. Charlie Allcorn was well-known all over the neighbourhood, particularly so as an auctioneer in the true style of that vocation.   [JT

10

A photograph that appeared in 'Keep's Illustrated Guide to Dunstable' of 1930, originally by Chas. Smy. Dunstable cross-roads at ten o'clock in the morning, looking down High Street North, policeman on point duty. Local buses are lined up on the right, drivers having a chat. The double-decker in front, outside Lloyd's bank, belonged to a Mr. Salter and was one of his 'Ideal' buses. The bicycle on the left probably belonged to Mr. Tilley, the butcher, whose establishment dates back to 1926 and who is the sole remaining name of pre-war Middle Row. On the far corner, on the left, can be seen the cross-roads old type sign post. [LM

A companion photograph to the previous one. The cross-roads, High Street South to the left, showing a few shops in Middle Row (including Tilley's, instantly recognisable to-day), West Street and 'The Nag's Head', with the men lounging outside it, on the corner of High Street North. Behind the removal van are the old public urinals that 'graced' the corner of Ashton Street and, further along, the Frances Ashton Almshouses.

Central Café and the 'Whipsiderry' and, of course, the big banks.

But then came a sort of intermediate stretch that on the left-hand side going north went from the other corner of Albion Street to the near corner of Regent Street. It was not really the centre of the town, in our eyes and it was not the true High Street North, either. But it did contain the Palace Cinema, where the three shops now stand next to the Bingo Hall, and the former General Post Office, the facade of which has been kept. So for the citizens of Dunstable, with a population of 8,900 in 1924 and just over 10,000 ten years later, it was rather an important stretch! The Dunstable Borough Gazette shop and offices, with its large thermometer on a white background that advertised Stephen's Inks, started it off. A few doors down was the long hardware store belonging to Mr. Quick and then to Mr. Stevens, with shelves and drawers all over the place. Between the cinema (different films twice a week, changed Thursdays) and the Post Office was a largely forgotten row of shops which included W. A. Small's furniture store, W. G. Creamer – baker

Next to those the two shops belong to Mr. Ellis, the hairdresser (this shop has now been reconstructed in the Chiltern Open Air Museum at Chalfont St. Giles) and Miss Gaisford, 'Ladies' and Children's Outfitters'. I suspect that the gaiters I mention in a later chapter came from there.　　　　　　　　　　　　　　　　　　　　*[LM*

and confectioner (both Mr. Small and Mr. Creamer were well-known Dunstable names), O. Westnutt – Electrical Contractors and Wireless Receivers, and Eileen's Ladies Hairdressing salon. After the Post Office came trees and a big garden and a couple of large houses.

On the opposite side of this stretch of road was the entrance of Park Farm (yes a farm), Anderson the tailor ('Dunstable School – By Appointment', it said over the top, next to the school crest) and Dr. Binns' large, handsome, tesselated grey-stone house called 'The Lawns', which was set well back from the road, with a big open garden in front that was a carpet of aconites in early Spring. I used to look for those aconites, even as a small boy and tell father, when mother and I got back home, that 'the aconites are out'.

Dr. Binns' residence was next to Grove House, but the good doctor had a dispensary, the front wall of which was faced with flints (it could almost be called a gatehouse to 'The Lawns') between his actual home and Grove House. To look at Grove House was to see it more or less as

13

Looking down High Street North from the Town Hall, on a sunny market day. The first shop on the left, with its blinds down, is World Stores. Over on the right, next to the archway of 'The White Hart', is Flemons & Marchant. Further down the Teas sign on the blind is The Central Tea-Rooms. Next to the last blind of those four, partly hidden, is the white-pillared front of the old National Provincial Bank, which, many years later, was to merge with the Westminster. The Old Sugar Loaf Hotel can be clearly seen. The first trees on the right are in Dr. Binns' garden, but there are also trees on the left-hand side of the road, shortly after passing the corner of Albion Street.

[LM

The fig tree growing out of Dr. Binns' dispensary. The doctor's house lay back on the right. Grove House in this photograph had become the Municipal Offices.   [P.C.(DS)

it stands today, but in the corner of the dispensary, right by Grove House, a fig tree came virtually out of the wall, spreading its branches over the pavement, so that the figs in season were very tempting. It was a Dunstable landmark, that fig tree.

The aconites and the fig tree therefore will be remembered by many older Dunstablians. But there were two other shops that dwell in my memory on that side of the High Street, in that intermediate stretch, which are worth recording. The other side of Dr. Binns' plot there was a barber's shop sunk below ground level. To get to it (and the dentist's next door) was a case of going through a little gate in the iron railings and down a steep flight of stone steps. Strangely the barber was a Mr. Barber. At one time I used to be taken there to have my hair cut, sitting on the stool that all small boys had to sit on, placed on the proper chair. Mr. Barber ('Tammy' Barber) was a little man with a round face and a wax moustache, with black, well-cut hair (naturally) smarmed down. Looking back now he was the epitome of the fourth man standing at the end of the row in a Barber's Shop Quartet. . . .

The second shop to mention was a general outfitters next but one to the Sugar Loaf. I remember it more as Seldon's, but before that it was Knight's. The point about this store, which mother seemed to frequent (and therefore I frequented, because if mother went up the town in my early days then I had to go, too) was that it had those marvellous little caskets on a ceiling railway that ran round the shop to deal with the money. When the bill had been made out the assistant reached up, took the lower half of the casket down off the wires, placed the money and the bill inside and screwed back the half so that the whole casket was replaced on the 'rail'. A cord would then be pulled and the whole thing would zoom around the wires, crashing through junction points until it came to the cashier sitting in a little glass compartment. She would take out the money, put in any change and the initialled bill and send the whole thing crashing back again. I used to stand there mesmerised. I longed to have a go, but I could never summon up enough courage to ask.

So High Street North for us really began at Regent Street with the big houses and porches that still stand, through Winfield Street – Union Street – Clifton Road – Waterlow Road – Chiltern Road – Beale Street and on to the lower railway station, under the bridge that no longer exists and to the corner of Brewers Hill. This was a long unmade track that went over the level crossing, past fields and meadows, past the farmhouse and buildings of Mr. Cook's Brewers Hill Farm on the right (where children now enjoy the small recreation ground and where opposite stood a brick mill-like building which I think must have been used as a grain store or something similar – anyway I always used to know it as a mill and it was one of my landmarks) until it reached the junction of Green Lanes. On the opposite side of our High Street North was the long stretch of Dunstable Grammar School, of blessed and happy memory, now Ashton Middle School. After that came a few shops, many houses (a number of them large ones with several storeys), several short roads that led down to the different gates of Waterlow's, under the bridge again and to the corner of Houghton Road, on the other side to Brewers Hill. Beyond Brewers Hill and Houghton Road lay the Chalk Cutting and Sewell, places to delight a small boy as he grew up and began to ramble around the countryside.

We did include Dog Kennel Path in *our* High Street North, in fact it was an important part of my scene, initially because it was there that I have the first memory of walking with my father, as a small boy of three, on a hot sunny Sunday morning. Dog Kennel is the path that leads off the main road between the present Ashton Middle School and Grove House gardens and is still traversed as a short cut between Dunstable and Houghton Regis. But in the twenties and thirties it was a far more pleasant and lovely walk than it is today. It was bordered by old railings for its first part. On the right lay the private grounds behind Grove House, belonging to the Bagshawe family and which were only opened to the public on a rare fête day, by courtesy of the owner. So the wooden fence that shielded those gardens precluded any view.

On the left was the edge of the Grammar School grounds – the strip behind the Science Buildings, the gymnasium and the woodwork room. Here were the big chestnut trees where in later years I was to play 'conkers' with form-mates. Then came the mysterious extremity of

Waterlow's factory, and then – delight, delight, as a little boy holding father's hand on those nostalgic mornings of long ago – the tiny wooden footbridge that went over the single track railway line that meandered through the small cutting from Luton to Dunstable. After that an open meadow and cornfields, all the way down to Houghton, with views across open countryside to the right. No factories, no scars on the landscape, no noise. Skylarks singing on high and the scents of summer.

It was a gentle walk of sun and dappled shade. By the wayside, just the other side of the footbridge, on a triangular grassy portion bordered by a small hedge where the softly-coloured dog roses grew in June, and by the side of the corn, whispering in the summer breeze, we looked for wild flowers and I was taught their names – scabious, which has always remained a favourite wild flower, toadflax, purple thistles, lady's slipper, pink and mauve vetches and kidney vetch, campion, ox-eye daisies, buttercups across the grassy meadow. Once upon a time there were corncockles in that cornfield and scarlet pimpernel and bright-eyed speedwell along the edges. . . .

I have digressed, which I suspect will not be the only time. But what are recollections if the person who is remembering them cannot do this from time to time? It is much more interesting to shoot off down the byways than always traverse the straight road. So whilst we are on the byways let us take time out for just a moment and refer to Union Street, which was one end of our home stretch of High Street North.

Union Street to me was different from the other side roads in that it seemed almost like a main thoroughfare and it went somewhere. You couldn't see the end of it, whilst if you stood at the bottom of Regent Street and Winfield Street and the pleasant tree-bordered Clifton Road and Waterlow Road and George Street and Park Street, all nearby roads, the tops could be seen. There was a finish to them all.

Union Street was a long street of small cottages and terraced houses, with odd small shops here and there and it stretched away until it reached Chiltern Road, at which point I can still visualise that road as a muddy track. The back streets that ran parallel to the High Street and started at West Street came out at Union Street, so it led to them, too. It was the street that I was taken up to go to Mr. & Mrs. Pickering's house in West Parade at Christmas time, it was the street that I would go up with father to Mr. Robinson's nurseries or be sent to get extra milk from Mr. Mooring, it was the street that led onwards to the Downs and other adventures.

It also had one very interesting building – a small tin tabernacle. Well, it wasn't really a tabernacle in the true sense of the word, but the building rather lent itself to this name – in fact it was known as the Tin Tabernacle – although it was really Christ Church. It stood between Stuart Street and Victoria Street on the right-hand side going up from the High Street. It also had an interesting story.

Apparently, around 1860, the good people of this northern end of Dunstable wanted to have a small church of their own, rather than make their way to the Priory. Union Street at that time (and in fact until 1961) divided the parishes of Dunstable on the south side of the street and Houghton Regis on the north side. So the citizens asked the then Rector of Dunstable if they could have a church on the south side, but the Rector didn't want to know. So they turned to the Vicar of Houghton Regis to see if he would have them in his parish. The Vicar was highly delighted so to do and thus Christ Church was built on the north side of Union Street. It served the community for nigh on eighty years, when in 1938 a plot of land was given to the church almost on the corner of Clifton Road (still in the Houghton parish) and a new more striking church was built.To bring the story of the tin tabernacle to a conclusion, the Army used it for storage in the last War and it was then pulled down.

To return to the straight road – Watling Street – and the confines of the shop itself and to the immediate circle and vicinity of my early days. Next to our shop on the right of it as you turned toward the afore-mentioned Union Street, was a kind of hat shop, very plain, with old matting on the floor and one wooden counter. It belonged to a Mrs. Dixon and a Mrs. Gravestock, who was Mrs. Dixon's daughter. They were, in fact, hat renovators and hats would be renovated on the premises, using an old block and steam iron. They were part, really, of the old local hat trade. The two ladies' husbands worked elsewhere but it is fair to say that we hardly knew the Dixons as neighbours at all – they were a very anonymous couple. Mr. & Mrs. Gravestock I do remember, they were both small persons and they seemed to be the only two of the neighbours, plus their daughter, that we saw or heard at all at that time. Mainly it was really a case of hearing Mrs. Gravestock. However, I was not really aware of them all that much. Later neighbours, yes – they were very much part of my growing-up and assisted my daily content-ment considerably, as will be seen.

The other side of this 'hat' shop were two big houses with bay windows and then a much larger one, known as Watling House. This was a double-bayed house, with a centre door, which was a boarding or lodging house. Outside it had the sign with the spoked wheel of the Cyclists Touring Club and it was used by commercial travellers. When A.C. Sphinx came to the town and built their new factory on the fields the other side of Brewers Hill a number of their personnel were put up there until they became established. After Watling House came a few cottages, before the wall was reached that sheltered the long yard of 'The Bull' public house on the corner of Union Street.

The house next but one to our house was inhabited by a builder and plumber by the name of Higgs. Henry Higgs. I have no idea what he looked like, but I do remember a Mr. Hawker, an electrician who followed. But either from this house or the one next to that there came a daily episode that sums up, really, the distant life of those days in the late twenties.

Every morning, when it was fine, around eight o'clock, there came two geese, who turned left at the end of their sideway, walked along the pavement in front of our shop to the corner of Clifton Road, around fifty yards in all. There they turned left and waddled up that road for another few yards until they reached a lane that ran along the back of the properties facing the High Street. We had a gate leading into this back way in the tall corrugated iron fence that marked the limit of our garden. Along this lane the geese went, turned right where it met Charlie Smy's big garden and carried on up until reaching a small grass field that lay at the back of the houses in Stuart Street, a turning toward the top of Clifton Road. Into that field they waddled and there they stayed for the day.

The point about this story is that they were completely unescorted. They knew the way and once they were let out, off they went of their own free will. No-one molested them, they were in no danger whatever and it was all a matter of routine. They must have come back, of course, later in the day and I suspect they were summoned for that journey according to the weather and the time available to their owner. I never seemed to see them return, but their outward preamble was a notable start to the day.

On the left of our shop, tucked next door, was a small single lock-up shop belonging to Mr. J. H. Abell, who lived down the bottom of Ashton Road. Then came our garden gate, then a wooden fence bordered by trees that stretched along to Mr. Grover's house and his motor-garage round the corner of Clifton Road. No row of shops – they came at a later date. Behind Mr. Abell's lock-up shop was part of our garden, behind the fence and trees a tennis court alongside the back of Mr. & Mrs. Grover's house. My sister, Eileen, who was twelve years older than I was, and her friends more or less had carte-blanche of that tennis court in the Grover's garden and in turn I had use of it in the same way, with my friends, whilst it existed.

Mr. Grover did not sell petrol at pumps, he was a motor mechanic and a dealer in second-hand cars. I can never really remember that corner without visualising the dim recesses of the garage itself and Mr. Grover with dirty hands, in his overalls. I rarely saw him at any other time, but I do know that that tennis court brought hours of pleasure to a lot of young people and I hope Mr. & Mrs. Grover knew that.

It was a peaceful little stretch of road, really, that portion between Union Street and Clifton Road – and I say that in spite of the fact that it was the main road to the north and to London, with heavy lorries

My father's shop and Mr. Abell's lock-up shop. The name of Abell is still retained on the present-day shop, but any family connection has long since gone.

Helping our assistant, Frank Fairhurst, to carry things into the shop. Ashton Road, Flinte House on the corner, stretches away. I was always happy to be around the shop, but sometimes got banished for getting myself in the way.

trundling through by day and by night. Yet it was peaceful – bicycles could be propped up on the kerb for a whole day, goods could be unpacked on the pavement from large packing cases and brought into the shop or the sideway, people would stop and talk without hindrance to passers-by. And I used to stand outside the shop as a small boy, in perfect safety, to watch 'Waterlow's' go by.

Waterlow & Sons, who had come to Dunstable in 1891, dominated the neighbourhood and in fact were the largest employer in the town, with 1500 people assured of steady work. Their buildings stretched from the borders of High Street North to the edge of the railway and they were indirectly responsible for a great part of the development of the northern end of the town, in that area. They had a fire engine of their own, the employees had their own swimming pool and the factory had a large chimney – at least by the standard of those days. And above all, they had a hooter.

That hooter could be heard all over the town. In fact, when the wind was in the right direction, it could be heard as far as Toddington. So to me, a hundred yards or so distant, it was a very loud hooter. It used to go off at five to eight and eight o'clock in the morning, one o'clock for lunch, five to two and at two for return to work and six o'clock for the

Waterlow & Sons, Ltd. – the Factory. A photograph taken from the 1933 'Official Guide to Dunstable and District'. [DD

21

end of the day. The two hooters at five minutes to the hour were the warning ones to the workers as they hurried to work and dead on the hour, when the second hooter went, the big gates of the George Street entrance would close. If any employee did not make it, then he or she was sent home. Retribution was instant.

My standing-out time to watch all the workers go by in their hundreds, was at lunch-time. Sometimes in the evening again, but nearly always the lunch-time, as they went home for their dinner, up the High Street and into all the surrounding little streets. Many of them were walking, of course, but a lot were on bicycles and some on motor bikes – rip-roaring, noisy machines that weaved their way in and out of the traffic. One such rider on a BSA I used to cheer as he went by. I came to know a lot of those Waterlow's people by sight and would look for them individually. They in turn would smile at me.

Later on I came to know the son of the Managing Director of the firm and for a period used to play in the garden in the house just inside the main gates. We also seemed to have the freedom of the area outside the house, which I rather think was forbidden territory. But to me Water-low's will always be the people going home for their mid-day dinner, streaming along the road and the pavements, and the big hooter sounding off its time of the day.

I have mentioned J. H. Abell and Charlie Smy. They were two of the characters of the home area and there were others too. Opposite the shop, between Ashton Road and George Street and going left, there was first of all a row of fairly large terraced houses, the last of which was a dentist's – Charles Hinton. He was a tall man who walked very quickly, very upright and generally with a homburg hat on his head. He was a leading light in the local Operatic & Dramatic Society. It was into Mr. Hinton's short front garden, one morning, that a runaway horse bolted, having got rid of its milk cart, tearing down Clifton Road and across the main High Street. Mercifully it missed any traffic, the horse fortunately was not hurt, but the patient in the dentist's chair was even more frightened than normal.

Next to this last house and through to the corner of George Street were four small shops. The first, at no. 110, belonged to Chas. Smy – Photographer. Obviously to me he was Mr. Smy, but he was really Chas. Smy because that is how he signed all his portraits. Chas. Smy for many years had been and was the well-known town photographer. For weddings, special occasions, portraits, groups, town scenes – Chas. Smy was the man.

He must have been one of Dunstable's characters, let alone our area of High Street North. He was a little man, with an equivalent little wife, although she extended her height a bit by wearing a large Edwardian hat with the customary Edwardian hat pins. Chas. Smy was also very dapper, with a benign smile, twinkling eyes and small tufts of hair at the side of his head. He was a kind of poor man's Robertson Hare, without quite the dome or the expressive voice. But when he disappeared behind the black cloth of his tripod camera, he almost did disappear, until all of a sudden there was the smiling face and a hand held high and flash would go the picture.

He must have taken thousands of photographs for people and organisations in and around Dunstable and his premises must have been one of the first in Dunstable to receive electricity in that he had his own generator. His shop had that strangely evocative smell of an old photography shop, with its little glass counter and portraits round the walls. In the inner sanctum was his studio, with its hanging drapes, an aspidistra, pedestals and ornaments. A complete contrast to the large open garden that Chas. Smy and his wife enjoyed at the end of our back lane and into which sometimes we had a peep. Courteous, kind, smiling, Mr. & Mrs. Smy, part of a generation that no longer exists.

Mr. Wilderspin's draper's shop was the next one along, absolutely full of items, including a variety of wools, with seemingly not an inch of room anywhere. Mr. Wilderspin was a stocky, short man, who bounced along and his son, whom I came to know in my 'teens, also was short and stocky.

Then came Christopher Knight. Mr. Knight had a little café, a very tidy, decorous place with a few round tables, which lent itself more to afternoon tea than other meals, but I suppose it caught the Waterlow's trade and other people passing by at that end of the town. Mr. Knight was a pleasant man, with a quiet, pleasant wife, but I remember him in particular for two things. Well, three really. He had a quiff of fair hair falling over his forehead and he spoke in a very high voice, totally unlike anyone else I knew. But the most important thing about Mr. Knight was his home-made ice cream.

It is one of my very earliest memories, being taken across on a summer (only in summer, you didn't have ice-cream at any other time of the year) Thursday afternoon – early closing day for the majority of shops – by my father, out of the garden gate, over the road to Mr. Knight's shop for a penny ice-cream cornet. On very special occasions, a twopenny one. That ice-cream was delicious and no other ice-cream, even from the blue and white chequered container on the bicycles belonging to Mr. Wall, or later from Mr. Eldorado, could match it. I can taste the flavour to this day and it was one of my high spots of the week. Once, to my anguish, I dropped the cornet just outside our gate, on the way back. I cried bitterly, but there was no return journey for another one. Quite rightly (thoughts of later years, of course, not at the time!) a lesson had to be learnt.

The last shop on the corner was a butcher's, but we bought our meat

23

Mr. F. H. Brookes, in a quieter
moment. /BB

from Mr. Brookes, who used to hold sway to one and all in his shop, mid-way between Winfield Street and Union Street, right opposite the arched entrance of the Grammar School. Frederick Harold Brookes was a strong non-conformist of distinct views on a number of subjects. He would stand at the back of his counter, sharpening his butcher's knife as only he could sharpen it, with considerable flair, whilst he greeted each customer by name in a loud voice and then, having ascertained their wants, proceed to carry out the order whilst having a running one-sided conversation on a particular subject. He would have made a wonderful ring-master in a circus, an entrepreneur of the first order. But he kept a clean, immaculate shop, sawdust on the floor and served the community with good honest produce, one of Dunstable's many notable shop-keepers. He was considerate to his customers and sincerely sympathetic to those in trouble. Freddie Brookes will be well remembered by those who knew him and it is interesting to note that his son, who was one of my early playmates, there being only two months difference in our ages, carried on the same trade in a small village in the delectable Duchy of Cornwall.

Coming back to 131 High Street North, on the other corner of Ashton Road stood Flinte House, named simply because the face of it was covered in flints. (Why the nondescript building that now stands there is named Queen's Court whilst Flint Court, without the 'e', is on the other side of the road, near 'The Bull' is beyond my simple comprehension). As such it had a character look about it. The sign outside this building indicated Campbell, Graves and Cox and it was a men's outfitters ('Up-to-the-minute style in Ladies & Gents wear' said the advertisement),

The result of the accident to Flinte House. A small crowd inspects the damage the following morning.

Repairs under way. Business as usual, says the notice board.

but what happened to Messrs. Campbell & Graves is a mystery to me, as I knew it when only Mr. Cox was there.

One afternoon a motor-cyclist came to grief outside Flinte House, going an awful head-over-heels tumble and finishing up yards ahead of his machine. To the surprise of those who witnessed it, the cyclist got to his feet and apart from the odd scratch and bruise the major damage was a severly torn pair of trousers. It was Mr. Cox who took him in, cleaned him up and saw that he had another pair of trousers to go on his way.

Not so fortunate was an accident that happened late one evening in the winter. There was a tremendous crash outside. A lorry driver travelling south had nodded off and crashed into the corner of Flinte House, severely damaging the ground floor and leaving the front bedroom exposed completely to view. Mercifully, Mr. & Mrs. Cox were in London on a theatre outing with a coach party and only heard of the mishap when police met the coach in at The Square on its return to Dunstable.

Another accident, right outside our shop, was when another lorry-driver, again at night, went into the big, tall telegraph post directly opposite and brought that down, with wires trailing all over the place.

Alongside Flinte House, behind a wooden fence, was part of the garden. Then, standing back, came three shops before 'The Wheat-sheaf' public house was reached. One of these shops was a confection-ers, the second belonged to Mr. Parsons. If Mr. Smy was the foremost character on one side of Ashton Road then George Parsons was most certainly the character on the other.

Mr. Parsons had two fronts. In the front, literally, of his house and building was his newsagent's shop, manned by his good lady, who

After the accident to the telegraph pole – work in hand. The corner house with the attractive attic extension was lived in by Mr. Hill, a vet. The next door house is for sale. I don't know whether this was the occasion or not, but at one time people came to live there from Scotland. They found Dunstable so cold in the winter that they fled back north.

before she became Mrs. Parsons was a Miss Proverbs. There must be the basis of a sermon in that, somewhere. (Mrs. Parsons herself was wont to say that she was the fifth proverb). Actually the whole place belonged for many years to Mr. Proverbs and having married one of his daughters Mr. Parsons later took over the complete business. The shop contained a considerable variety of papers, periodicals, magazines, small books and annuals. It was also a not inconsiderable stationers, with all sorts of side lines. In fact there was a lot for sale in that shop and we frequented it, often. It was so easy to 'pop across to Parsons' and pop across to Parsons we did, at all hours of the day.

But I suppose George Parsons will be remembered, from a trade point of view, for the other side of his business, at the back of the shop and actual house. Here was his printing 'establishment'. Here, assisted by his eldest son, Mr. Parsons would be found in the midst of what appeared to be the most incredible jumble ever to be seen, in a small building literally jammed full of printing material, relevant or irrelevant. Round the old-fashioned actual printing machine was a seemingly untidy heap of trays of type, old founts, quoins, engravings, shelves stacked with bits of paper, hung posters and bills, coloured cards, pieces of this and pieces of that. The walls, the ground, the bench, the shelves,

Mr. & Mrs. George Parsons.
/BP

the drawers, the ceiling were all stacked or covered by a mind-boggling variety of objects. That any sense could ever come out of such a scene was surely too much to expect.

But sense did and Mr. Parsons, being also an improviser, catered well and fairly to all those organisations – churches, sports clubs, service organisations, political bodies, tradesmen, charities, the arts and a host of other persons who wanted notices, programmes, tickets, bills, letter-headings, announcements, etc. etc. done reasonably cheaply and without fuss. He had a wide market and in a town where a number of odd back-street printing houses could be found, George Parsons reigned supreme, carrying out orders that the bigger establishments, such as Index and Enterprise, were too busy on another footing to do.

A man of smallish stature, I am not being unkind when I say that he could melt into a crowd and not be seen. A strong Primitive Methodist, he served the Victoria Street church well and steadfastly and with his kindly wife, who had an understanding of a small boy waiting impatiently for the latest Japhet and Happy Annual to come in (yes, I was an Arkub!) he took his place as a friendly person in my formative years.

The other side of 'The Wheatsheaf' and by the side of the first entrance to the Grammar School, there used to be two other very small shops, with the living accommodation again over and behind. They have long since gone which, for one in particular, is a pity as it was a good example of a children's sweet shop – really a tuck shop. The other was a drug-store (at one time a chemist's associated with the afore-mentioned

27

Mr. Hinton) and in both cases the person entering had to go down a step. In the case of the sweet shop anyone tall had to duck their head, too.

In this sweet shop was another character, looking after a character shop. 'Daddy' Barnes. His name really was Oswald Barnes and to be correct this shop and this person did not really come into my life until late 1933, when I started at the big school, but I include it now because it was part of the locality that was mine. To all us boys who frequented that shop, before school, in the lunch hour or after school, the owner was and always will be 'Daddy' Barnes, although to my knowledge he had no children.

'Daddy' Barnes was another little man, on a height level with Chas. Smy. He was very undistinguished-looking really, thin with a little moustache and very little hair on top. He was never *in* the shop when you were the first one to enter, he always came in, in his waistcoat, no top coat, from the dim recesses of a back room. I never saw him outside the shop, in the town or anywhere, over the years. As far as I was concerned, and later I was to find out that he also ran a Business Transfer Agency, he existed in the shop and as long as the shop stood he was a fixture in it.

Great were the enticements on display. Sticks of liquorice, orange 'shoe-laces', gob stoppers that changed colour as they were eaten (several times, they had to be taken out of the mouth to be looked at every now and again) and could be had for one farthing each (*one farthing*, oh that lovely British coinage), sherbert dabs, aniseed balls, bulls-eyes, clove sweets, jubes, wine gums, fruit bon-bons, milk drops, 'Bluebird' and Sharpes' toffees, jelly babies. We never went, of course, for the up-market items like Toblerone and Fry's crunch, but basically for the cheapest and in some cases the most primitive. There were also bottles of fizzy drinks – Tizer to the fore.

'Daddy' Barnes would wait patiently (or was it sometimes impatiently?) whilst we chose, take our money and then slip back into his room again as we went out of the door. He must have seen a whole generation or more of Dunstable Grammar School boys. I know a whole generation must remember him.

I mentioned earlier, Brookes the Butcher (put like that it sounds rather like 'Happy Families'. . .). Along that varied row of shops 'twixt Winfield and Union Streets, there was also Wild's. This shop sold games and sports equipment and leather goods and was also a saddlery. It was managed by one, Sammy Taylor, although for many years, quite understandably, I thought he was Mr. Wild. For several reasons that shop was important to me.

First, it was where we purchased card games and board games. My parents were happy to play a game in the evening, if time and work permitted, or at weekends, so 'Lexicon' was bought there and 'Counties of England' and 'Speed' and 'Pit' (although this really needed five at least to make it really exciting) and 'Can-U-Go' in the card variety. The board games covered 'Peggity', 'Sorry' (which we played a lot and which I still have, every now and again brought into use), 'Halma' and one called 'Ho-Mo', which was advertised as 'The New Soccer Football Game' and had a board with lots of black and white small squares, twenty-two little wooden counter men, a miniature football and dice. 'Fireside Football' was another in this category and I sat at the table with father and we played imaginary matches with imaginary teams, without a lot of success if I remember rightly. My first (and only, now I come to think about it) chess set came from Wild's, as did a set of draughts.

Then there were jigsaws, which the whole family enjoyed and I started doing at an early age. Trains going through the countryside; ships at sea; animals on the farm; seaside scenes; huntsmen and horses; gentlemen in coloured waistcoats sitting by a roaring fire with food on a side table, a grog in hand and dogs at the feet; one on the Cathedrals of England, which for some reason I particularly recall. Sometimes we had a really big and difficult jigsaw which we put out on a table in our through room and which we were inclined to stop at and insert a piece here and there as we journeyed through the room to the shop or upstairs.

The second reason for my association with Wild's was when I started playing 'proper' games and it became my venue for buying sports equipment. Thus my first football boots came from there, an early cricket bat, a hockey stick, table-tennis (ping-pong really at that age) bats and net, a tennis racquet and balls of all kinds.

So a rapport sprang up between Mr. Taylor and myself, a rapport that became very strained one morning when I was around twelve or thirteen. Mr. Taylor, who incidentally always wore a sort of khaki-coloured shop coat when he was serving, kept a very clean shop (as did nearly all the traders and furthermore they swept the pavement in front of their shops every morning and *washed it down* frequently, too) and three times a week at least he washed his linoleum floor with a mop and a pail of water. I bounded in one morning early, bent on a message to obtain something for the school, just as he had completed the operation. I did not notice the bucket of dirty water just inside the shop door and sent it flying. Sammy Taylor wasn't too pleased. . . .

The third reason for my sojourns to that shop was the annual pilgrimage to get my fireworks. That was always one of the days of the year. Standard fireworks were my favourite make and although I might put up with the odd one from Brocks, it was Standard I bought. I knew what I wanted, I would point my finger and call out their names. Mr.

Taylor would reach inside the glass case that ran along the top of his long counter, put them in a bag for me and I would go home rejoicing. I lingered over that moment of buying fireworks and Mr. Taylor humoured me. A couple of Snow-Storms, a Chrysanthemum Fountain, a Rising Sun, a Roman Candle, a couple of small rockets (large ones were too expensive), Golden Rains and Silver Rains to hold in the hand, a bunch of Sparklers, two or three jumping crackers, a Catherine Wheel (only one, it never seemed to go round properly when it came to it), a Haley's Comet, a Volcano, a Mount Vesuvius, a Jack-in-the-box, the odd squib . . . so I could go on. Once my Uncle Ted and Auntie Ethel (father's sister), who came down from Abbey Wood twice a year, were staying with us at the end of October and Uncle Ted, whom I always liked and who was the one that took me to my first football match at Luton (Luton Town v Aldershot, Luton won 2–1), bought me a half-crown box of Standard fireworks. A half-crown box! What joy, what ecstasy!

In that row of shops was also 'The Hat Shop', owned and run by Mrs. Edith Rule. Actually it was a bit more than a hat shop, although it was called that. Ladies' Millinery – sold, renovated, re-modelled, made, went along with the title and Mrs. Rule fitted that shop admirably. She *was* The Hat Shop, moving her ample frame in a stately way, at a slow pace and talking to and advising her customers in a refined and educated voice. She would not have been out of place in the millinery shops of the centre of London. Mother used to buy her hats there, preferring it to Miss Wilson's hats, which were stuck on thin pedestals in the window in front of a green curtain in a shop the other side of the alleyway to Cycles & Wireless. So, of course, I was dragged in there early on in life, because there would be no-one to look after me at home. I would listen in a bored way to Mrs. Rule expounding her ware. She must have made an impression on me to remember her well now. But then Mrs. Rule was a lady among gentlemen shopkeepers and they were a rare species for a main high street at that time – the Mrs. Rules and the Miss Wilsons and the Misses Omer and Harlow of this world.

Apart from my mother and father and my sister I suppose the first persons that I came to know and recognise were my father's assistant in the shop, Frank; the errand boy of the time; Mrs. Mustill, a friend of my mother's who came to be known as Auntie Fannie and Mr. & Mrs. Abell.

Both the Abells were close and good friends of my mother and father and they had known one another from the first days of my family coming to Dunstable. Mr. Abell (the 'J' of the J.H. was really John, but he was always called Jack by his close associates) was a Devonian by birth and he brought with him to this corner of Bedfordshire the salt air and the rich country soil of his native county. He had a wooden leg, his own having been injured in some road accident, so that he walked with a pronounced limp. Of average height and well-built, he held forthright views and was not afraid of voicing them. He was often bluff and could, at times, be a little fearsome in a small boy's eyes, but he was a kind man and would listen as well, often chuckling away at any antics that amused him.

Mr. Abell, after some years as a coalman, became a wireless engineer in the still early days of wireless and in the compact square lock-up shop, consisting of the shop itself, a small office and a back repair room, he mended wirelesses, did a busy trade in the exchange of accumulators and sold his radio and electrical goods over the counter. He drove a large, powerful, Royal Enfield motor-bike with side chassis. On the chassis he either put a normal passenger side-car, when he wanted to transport Mrs. Abell, or a big storage container with another small, sloping one in front. They would hold all his wireless equipment etc. required for his visits to and from customers. On these containers in large lettering were his name and telephone number and the fact that he gave a Wireless Service. It was his trademark and Mr. Abell with his motor-bike combination was a familiar figure in both town and village.

Mr. Abell brought to his everyday work a strong faith and there were very few Sundays when, as a local preacher of some note, he would not be preaching the Gospel at one of the seventeen chapels that made up the circuit of the Methodist Church on The Square. If he was not appointed either morning or evening, then he and his wife would be in the back pew at the mother church. In some ways he was an old-fashioned man of old-fashioned ways. In others he was abreast and ahead of the times.

I remember helping him, early on, unload big packing cases that had been dumped on the pavement by the kerb and I think he was happy to have me around, as he had no children of his own. On bank holidays the Abells and my parents would often have picnics together, Mr. Abell using his motor-bike for transportation in some way or another. The liaison was close and I know my father often used to tell him about visitors to our shop, including the travellers representing the various firms.

That fact led to an embarrassing incident at one time for Mrs. Abell, who unlike her husband, unfortunately had no real sense of humour, one of life's priceless assets. The travellers who came round were often the same persons, year after year and they were sometimes known to my father, who got on well with them and *did* have a sense of humour, by some kind of mannerism or speech. Thus, because of his syrupy voice, the very polite and well-dressed man from Hartley's (jams and jellies) was known as 'Mr. Raspberry'. On this particular occasion this gentle-man – and I have no idea what his proper name was, and I am not at all

'Helping' Mr. Abell with the packing cases. Wireless batteries stand around on the pavement. A little girl watches from across the road. The two shop blinds further along belong to Mr. Smy and Mr. Wilderspin. On the opposite corner of George Street, just past the car, is a big house, altered when Mr. Herington, the chemist of High Street South and another Dunstable worthy, built his second shop in 1934, so having one at each end of the town.

Mr. Abell's work horse. Mr. Abell driving, my mother behind, Mrs. Abell sitting on top with the figure in the grey felt hat eating an ice-cream. This photograph taken at Ashridge on one of our bank-holiday outings.

sure that my father knew either, or perhaps through use of the nickname he had forgotten it – enquired about something he wanted to buy
from a wireless merchant. Did father know the trader next door that
well? So father took him in to see Mr. Abell, to find Mrs. Abell in the
shop as well. He introduced his companion to the Abells as the traveller
for Hartley's jams. "Good morning", said Mr. Abell. "Oh, hello, Mr.
Raspberry" said Mrs. Abell. I ask you. . . .

For some reason or other, although it was part of our High Street
North, the other side of Clifton Road and George Street opposite, going
north, did not have quite the same meaning for me. I suppose really it
was because, unless it was a walk down to Sewell or over the path on top
of the Chalk Cutting, or an occasional train to be caught at the lower
station (most of our transport was by bus), we didn't go down that way
much. Our journeying was mostly turn right out of the shop or up
Clifton Road itself.

Nevertheless our side of the road did have considerable character and
contained a lot of interest, much of which has completely disappeared,
like the second Christ Church building. There was the little LMS
station, with the wide, sloping drive-in which also acted as a turn round
for the green Eastern National buses. This station, the second of
Dunstable's two stations, marked the single track line from Dunstable
Town (LNER) to Leighton Buzzard, through the Sewell cutting and via
the halt at Stanbridgeford. There were three public houses – 'The
Spread Eagle', 'The Railway Hotel' and 'The Bird in Hand'; only the
last one remains and that is completely altered. There was Waterlow
Road Methodist Chapel, on the corner of Waterlow Road and that is
still there, virtually unchanged.

But the outstanding building down there, on the far corner of Chiltern
Road and opposite 'The Tower House', where Mr. J. T. Dales of the
world famous Dales' Dubbin (manufactured in a small factory in
Tavistock Street, close-by) lived, was the brewery. Bennett's Brewery.

*Mr. Dales himself, known locally as
J.T.D., was Mayor of Dunstable in
1919. His daughter, Lucy, followed
him in this position in 1925 and she has
a niche in local history as the first Lady
Mayor of the town.* [CDM

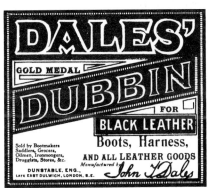

33

This was a real brewery, with a chimney and a wide entrance for brewers' carts pulled by big horses with big feet, and the smell that emanated from the brewery was the unmistakable smell of such establishments of that era. Alongside came the manager's house, standing back with a large front garden. Next to the house and as part of the Bennett establishment was a soda water factory, with the soda water sold in glass bottles with glass ball tops. Very few towns had a soda water factory and the interesting thing about this building was that it was originally the Railway Mission, which the Waterlow Road church replaced when it was built in 1905. Because of its origin Bennett's were not allowed to produce alcoholic beverage on the site, hence the soda water. (Incidentally, I understand that women who wanted to make their own bread would take a cup to the brewery for a pennyworth of yeast.)

To be truthful, neither the pubs nor the brewery played any part in my up-bringing, but they were there and therefore part of the scene, in particular the brewery. Which leads me, mentioning the horses, to recall that horses in the days that I used to watch the traffic go by, either from the shop door-step or from my parents' bedroom window, sitting on the wide window seat, were very much an integral part of the every-day movement of the High Street.

Apart from the brewer's dreys there were the coal merchants who stacked their carts with their big, strong sacks of coal from their sidings at the station, each merchant to his place. The driver, almost as dirty as the coal itself, used to sit up on a little seat above the horse to travel on his rounds. A nosebag would be fitted on the horse with fodder in it and the horse would delve into this at stopping places. The round finished, the horse and the empty, flat cart would be seen on the way down to the station again for another load.

We used to have our milk delivered each day by horse and cart. It would be ladelled out of big milk churns, all the way from a farm at Toddington. Mr. Withington used to bring it in, a tall, sad-looking man. Sometimes his wife would be with him, an even sadder looking person. Perhaps it was the fact that they were at the back of a horse for most of the day that made them look sad.

Another tradesman to use a horse was Mr. Smith, the baker in Church Street, the horse pulling a van which looked like a small version of the old type covered wagon, but which had doors at the back.

Every now and again a pony and trap would go by, the driver holding the reins from inside the cab, a long whip by his side. These were business trips, as well as the leisurely outing ones that were inclined to take place on a Thursday afternoon or on a Sunday. With all these horses about, there were a lot of droppings and each morning and afternoon a little man was employed to come along with bucket and

34

spade. Rich pickings.

However I cannot close this chapter without mentioning the changes that took place in our little strip of the High Street around 1935–36. The shop on our immediate right became a fishmongers. Mr. & Mrs. Grover moved away and all of a sudden there was no fence to the end of Clifton Road, no trees, no tennis court, and a row of shops sprang up. The lock-up shop became The Swan Lending Library, privately run by a genteel lady by the name of Mrs. Simper, and Mr. Abell built himself a bigger and more modern shop next door with accommodation over the top, as all the new shops had. The row included a wool shop, a hairdresser's (Mr. Wilcox) and on the corner, Barney Green the greengrocer.

Certainly the last-named added more character to the neighbour-hood. And I didn't mind the changes all that much. By then I could play tennis at school if I wanted to, even in the holidays. Mr. Abell was still nearby and the fact that we now had a library next door was a big plus. This opened up lots of paths and for twopence a book I could get all Richmal Crompton's William books, the Biggles yarns, Bulldog Drummond and other adventure stories. But something had changed, although I didn't realise it at the time.

So, overall, that was my composite area of Dunstable. Including the side roads and the back streets, it was a real community. The people and the scenes and the sounds conjured up in this reflective look come easily to mind, because they were all part of my growing-up years and they are never really forgotten. But all this was enhanced by the family and the garden and the place where I really did grow up, day by day.

Advertisement relating to the goodness of Bourne's bacon – from an August 1931 edition of the Dunstable Borough Gazette. [DG

A photograph, taken around 1938, full of interest. On the left David Sewell's fish shop, followed by my father's shop, The Swan Library, J. H. Abell and then along to the corner of Clifton Road, with the blind down over Barney Green's green grocery. Further along, the chimney of Bennett's brewery and right in the distance, beyond the railway bridge, the trees of Brewers Hill. Shop bicycles stand alongside the pavement, by the lamp post, and a Dunstable Corporation workman, with his cart, sweeps the gutter (that happened every morning at least). On the immediate left also, propped up against the house, a board advertising the films for that week at the Palace Cinema. On the right the telegraph pole that suffered mishap (or its replacement), the 'Teas' sign outside Christopher Knight's (of ice-cream delight) shop and opposite the brewery chimney, the topmost part of the striking 'Tower House', home of J. T. Dales. Mr. Dales' father, who had had the house built, was a keen astronomer and the turret seen here in the picture was his observatory. Perhaps the most fascinating part of this scene is the traffic, which consists of two cyclists, one on the wrong side of the road, and a lorry coming up in the distance! Oh! . . . and a pram.

Chapter 3

HOME AND GARDEN

When my father and mother came from Plumstead in 1919 together with my sister Eileen and also with my father's brother and his wife, who had no children, they must have thought they had come to live in a different world. They had lived all their lives in the confines of Plumstead and Woolwich, with its row upon row of small terraced houses and many narrow, tiny streets and with the hustle and bustle of an area dominated by the munitions factory of Woolwich Arsenal, where my father and his brother had worked.

Here, in this market town, in this south-west corner of Bedfordshire, they found tree-lined streets, a wide high street with interesting buildings and shops, big churches, a grammar school of some note, two railway stations, a character Town Hall. An historic place going back to the Romans, the early British and beyond, a Royal and Ancient Borough, peaceful and relatively calm. They knew nothing of the grocery trade, but they now had a shop that they owned, as their own masters, a big house in which to live, the size of which transcended by far anything they had ever experienced and a large garden area to work in, play in, enjoy and develop to their own liking.

On the doorstep was rolling countryside. True, where they had lived there was Plumstead Common and it was but a short walk to Bostall Woods, but here were the Downs, that edge of the Chiltern Hills looking out and over the shires of England, green, green lanes and quiet walks across meadows full of buttercups, over paths between waving corn and alongside hedges with Spring and Summer and Autumn colours. People to meet, to serve, to make friends with, a country community which compared with nothing that they had ever known.

The shop was first set up as Bourne Brothers (Bourne Bros. it said on the head-board) and by coincidence they began at this shop, on this important northern stretch of the Watling Street, fifty-four years after their grandfather (Pensioned Sergeant Charles Clark of the Royal

Artillery, late Principal Warder of Parkhurst Prison on the Isle of Wight), whom they never knew, was proprietor of a chemist's shop in Welling High Street, part of the old Dover road running from the City of London to Dover and which is the southern stretch of the self-same Watling Street.

My father, Edmund, and his brother, Charles, were twins. Look-alike twins. Not dead spitting images (although I have single photographs of them both in their early twenties and neither my sister nor I are sure which is which), but close enough that when together they drew a second look from the person seeing them to make sure if that person was seeing double – which of course was the case. Because they were twins of this nature they did, quite naturally, add to the character of the local community and were therefore characters in themselves as a result. There is one lovely story told of them, at a very early stage of their coming to Dunstable.

A lady customer, who either had not been in the shop before or who had not met the new owners, came in one day when my father was alone in the shop, just finishing serving another person, behind the grocery counter, on the right. That accomplished he turned to this lady and asked if she could possibly wait one moment, please, as he was needed in the house for a minute. As he went out of the right-hand door of the shop, which led to the house, and closed it, my Uncle Charlie came in at that exact second through what we called the yard door at the back of the left-hand side of the store. He came along the provision counter and said to the lady "Can I help you, Madam?" The lady took one look, clapped her hands to her head at this apparent sleight of body, shrieked and ran out of the shop at great speed. . . .

Uncle Charlie (another uncle for whom I had a lot of affection, although we did not see him that often in later years) and his wife, Auntie Flo, did not stay all that long. I would imagine the business was not really big enough to look after two separate branches of the family and Auntie Flo, apparently, was more a Londoner and was not all that happy with the quieter life of Dunstable. So they moved, after two or three years, for Uncle Charlie to set up his own grocery shop in Tolworth, Surrey, near Surbiton. So the Dunstable shop really became E. C. Bourne – Grocery & Provisions Merchant, although the Bourne Bros. head-board remained and the shop continued to trade as such for several years.

A house and garden that meant much to my parents, it was a wonderful place in which to grow up for a small boy. Built around 1906 it was a long, tall house, stretching backwards. There were no off-shoots downstairs, the rooms just came one after the other.

Behind the house shop door and in between that and another door were the stairs, very upright ones. Inevitably I fell down them one day

The twins – Uncle Charlie on the left, my father on the right.

from top to bottom, with a considerable crash. Doors opened from all directions in remarkably quick time, but aged five I had a bit of bounce on me and all was well. Nothing was damaged, injured or broken and mother could sit down and recover her breath, although it was not her breath that really needed recovering.

The other door led immediately into 'the best room'. For some peculiar reason it was called the dining room and I know not why, because we never ate there, apart from Sunday afternoon tea round the fire in winter. Later it did become the lounge and that was a better description, although even then it was not quite right as it was really a through room from the one we seemed to live in to elsewhere and vice-versa. But it was furnished a cut above the others, had a warm red and blue patterned carpet and at least it had a warm look, even though the draughts seemed to blow all around the floor. In the winter and in inclement weather Sunday afternoon and evening was spent there.

In the corner stood the upright family piano which mother used to play quietly, gently and sing gently, too. There was an attractive mahogany sideboard along the inner wall, in which was kept all the best linen, china, cutlery and glass ware, of which mother was very proud and which she looked after with great care. It was always clean, always polished, always sparkled. Opposite this, on the other side of the room and alongside the piano was the bay window looking out on to the yard, which ran along the whole length of the buildings. There were times when I hit one side of this bay window a resounding bang with a ball, but mercifully it never broke. It must have been very tough glass and well fitted.

At the end of this room, on the mantelpiece there stood, central and flanked each end, a French ormulu clock, with its side pieces. This had been my parents' wedding present to one another and it stood out from any other ornament or picture in the house. By the side of the wide fireplace, brass companion-set in place behind the encircling black fender, was a recess in which stood a very big, deep leather arm chair. There were other comfortable chairs in the room and a two-legged oak table, highly polished, stood, flaps down, in front of the window. Both doors in this room had a heavy curtain on a rail in front of them, which, when the room was in use, was pulled across to help eliminate draughts.

After the dining room came the hall, this really being the entrance to the house from the narrow covered sideway that ran off the High Street and alongside the shop into the yard. The outside door was a big one, polished beautifully and with a resounding knocker. In the hall were coat pegs and racks and a walking stick and umbrella stand one side and a big low cupboard-type piece of furniture the other side which went the whole length of the wall and was a great storage place. On its top stood the upright black telephone, with its ear-piece hanging on a hook. (Our telephone number was Dunstable 171, not a difficult number to remember compared with the six digits of to-day).

There were two deep massive drawers in this sideboard, above the actual cupboards and shelves. The left-hand one was allotted to me and in this, as time went on, I crammed all my bits and pieces that were not books or board games. All my cigarette cards, match box tops, stamps, and collections of this, that and the other were in there. My Dinky toys, pencils, rubbers, some of the card games, note-books, anything that I did not know where to put, were shoved in that drawer.

When I think of all those sets of cigarette cards that I once had I could weep. Footballers, cricketers, horses and jockeys, famous trains, birds, animals, butterflies and moths, wild flowers, Kensitas silk flags, film stars, soldiers, Kings and Queens of England, dogs, tennis players and their strokes – cards not only from cigarette packets but from tea packets as well. All done up in sets with a rubber band or carefully slotted into presentation albums. Oh dear, oh dear, oh dear! Swapping cards and making up a set was one of the delights of childhood. Now they are all gone to re-appear for princely sums at Antique Fairs or bric-a-brac shops. Oh my Players and my Wills of long ago!

After the hall came the living room, which really was a fairly small, square compact room with one up and down sash window looking out again on to the yard. Here we had all our meals and when I had a party, or on special occasions such as Christmas or on a Sunday when we had visitors, an extra leaf was put in the table. Father used to work on this table from his desk in the corner, particularly at the end of the week on a Saturday evening, when the shop takings were counted up for the week and the book-keeping done; mother used to put her Singer on it for any dressmaking or material work she was doing and eventually I used to do my prep on it. Apart from the upright table chairs, there was a small wicker-work chair that used to be a nursing chair and a couple of more comfortable easy chairs with arms.

A small fireplace gave us warmth in what was a really cosy room. By the side of the fireplace was a side oven that could be used for warming up dishes. In a dormer recess stood our wireless set, which by the time we changed it when I was about twelve, was somewhat ancient. It was used extensively for music and news and variety shows such as the Saturday night 'Music Hall', plus the football results, and there were times when the reception from it was not the best in the world. When we did eventually change it – and it was partly through my persuasion – I fiddled around with the new one for days on end, getting all sorts of stations like Luxembourg and Hilversum. I thought it was absolutely wonderful.

When I was in the house I spent a great deal of my waking life in that room. Food was eaten in it, games were played in it, books were read in it (one afternoon, reading a book in the chair in the corner, there was a growing rumbling and the ceiling above my head fell down on me), competitions were done in it, music was listened to in it, work was carried out in it, we sat and talked in it and visitors came and sat in it, too. And stories were told in it. My father shut up the shop for lunch, as was the custom for many shops. After the meal in winter or on wet days, he would sit in the corner and have his five minutes snooze. Then, when I was very young, he would pick me up and sit me on his lap and tell me a story. A made-up story.

He was a wonderful story teller and he had a story for each letter of the alphabet, often about a particular animal or bird. The favourite and I think the best was the one about Jacky the Squirrel, who went searching for wood-nuts, and it ended with a little song in which I could join. That story has come down the generations and has been told to my nephew and niece and to their children and now to my grand-children. But there was also the one about the Blue Bus; Larry the Lamb, who jumped on a goods train that stopped by his meadow and got carried away in a coal truck; Violet the Vulture; the Unicorn and the Fairies; Oswald the Ostrich; the reindeer, and, oh yes, the one about a quagga. Lovely, small children's stories, coming from an imaginative mind.

If father was the story-teller and the bread earner and the man of the house and many other things besides, mother was the one who looked after the home, kept it impeccably and produced all the meals. How she managed to cook all those meals so well and present them in such an appetising way from the small kitchen-scullery that led off the living room, I do not know. Yet she did and she never failed us, whether it was the normal day's routine, with a full breakfast, a hot meal at lunch time and afternoon tea, or Sunday lunch or some special event.

It was in this kitchen-cum-scullery at the end of the actual downstairs living quarters, although a cellar came off it, that all the weekly and daily washing was done, most of the ironing, and all the cooking. There was one small window and the back door, which led on to the yard, was left open on warm days. In the corner, by the window, until I was at least seven or eight, was one of those big coppers, covered by a wooden top. Here the washing was boiled on a Monday, stirred and lifted out with a round wooden stick, put through a mangle in a shed outside and, in the winter or if the day was wet, hung up on one of those old-fashioned wooden clothes racks, operated by a pulley, in the same room as the washing was done. It was a hard, grinding start to the week. When the copper eventually went, a better sink was put in, but it was still small for all the washing up and clearing up that had to be done.

A kitchen top, with a deep cupboard below on one side, where bread and cakes and flour were stored and with drawers on the other side for cutlery, stood against the wall and it was on this top that all the food was

One of the earliest photographs. My mother, sitting on the hammock that used to be strung up in the garden.

prepared. An old kitchen table by the door and an ordinary dresser on the inner wall completed the kitchen furniture, except for the all important gas stove, which was squeezed in between the table and the wall that gave way to the cellar. The floor was a stone one with, in the early days, rush mats.

There was, of course, absolutely none of the modern equipment that we see in the majority of housewives' kitchens to-day. No gadgets on the wall, no buttons to push, no quick serving area, nothing. Everything had to be done by hard work and the simple ordinary tools of the trade. Milk was kept in the cellar, as was the meat and ham. The cellar had steep stone steps and great care had to be taken particularly on the going down of those steps. It was an awkward descent with nothing to hold on to and we always treated those steps with the greatest respect. I might have whizzed round the rest of the house, but not down there,

Mother made a great point of meals, of good wholesome food, but she also had her specialities which included a number of delicious sweets. At Sunday lunch and when we had any guests at all she set a high standard and maintained that standard. Her laying of the table had to be to her perfection and in other circles she would have made a gracious and notable hostess. When all places had been laid, the spotless serviettes in their silver rings, the carvers placed on a pair of carving rests, the glassware sparkling and a jug of water or still lemonade put on a table that was covered with a clean, starched table cloth, it all looked so attractive. It was matched by the quality of the food and I have been exceedingly fortunate through life to have had first a mother, then a wife who followed those principles.

At the top of the stairs, by the side of the landing window that looked out over the lean-to roof which offered shelter immediately behind the shop, before the yard began, was a tiny box room, full of odds and ends including the old hammock, which was used in the garden in the early days. In the front of the house, above the shop, was my parents' large bedroom with its bay window. Then came my sister's room, which became mine when she was married in the summer of 1936 and left home. The top frontage and those two windows, viewed from Ashton Road, are exactly the same now as they were then.

After these two rooms the landing swung left to a corridor along the inner wall, with a small bathroom and another bedroom on the left. There was a step down to this corridor and it was not lit. To me, early on, it was a dark and fearsome corridor and if something was wrong with the light nearer the top of the stairs, which seemed to be often the case, it took a deal of courage to shoot along there to the safety of that bedroom, which was my first one and which was a very comfy square room. The window was the continuance of the double bay over the dining room below. A bed along the side wall, a small wardrobe with a glass panel, a big linen cupboard on the other wall, a tiny mantelpiece under which an electric stove stood that could warm up the room on winter nights, and scenes of Christopher Robin and Winnie the Pooh in pictures on the walls. Although I was just as far away as I could be from the downstairs living room, I was happy in that room, as I was also when I moved up to more senior status into the bigger room, which I was really able to make into a boy's bedroom.

All I can say about the bathroom was that it just had room for a bath, a toilet (with a rubber ball at the end of a chain), and a wash basin, all in clinical white – no colours in those days. At one time the bath had an old-fashioned geyser above it and great were the tribulations undergone to work that geyser successfully. A tiny window looked out over the lean-to and needless to say I had to be rescued one day through that window when I had bolted the door, against orders, and couldn't undo it.

At the end of the corridor was another bedroom, a big room in which any guests stayed. This was called the Rose Room and was always referred to as that, initially because of the old wallpaper covered in large pink roses. When this was scraped off and the walls distempered pink, the name naturally remained. It could have sounded rather grand to say to a guest – 'We've put you in the Rose Room', but mother and father were never like that and had no pretence to grandness whatsoever – they were completely the opposite.

The Rose Room was a spacious but ordinary room, although it did have one peculiar characteristic. Almost as though it had been added on afterwards there was an oblong 'bay' window, some 3 feet in depth and 8 feet in length which stuck out over the yard below. From here the line of the Downs could just be seen. I always thought this 'bay' looked somewhat precarious and I was never happy standing or sitting in a chair in it, although it was the sunniest spot in the house.

The kitchen/scullery on the ground floor and the guest bedroom on the top floor were the end of the living quarters, but it was not the end of the building. Then came the two big warehouses, strangely enough called the bottom warehouse and the top warehouse. They were linked by a set of interior wooden steps hugging the outside wall, but with no hand rail and a drop the other side. The entrance to the warehouses was, again, off the yard.

A lot of goods went into these warehouses for storage until brought into the shop. Those were the days when far more foods, etc. came in sacks and which then had to be weighed out. So the butter beans and haricot beans, the demerara sugar, sultanas and currants, dried apricots, prunes, dried peas etc. all had to be stored in a safe, dry place, as did the sacks of corn. Large cardboard cartons full of packets of cereal had to be emptied and stored as did wooden boxes containing tins of this, that and the other. In the top warehouse, there were racks round the walls, (on which we also used to lay our apples, picked from the two trees in the garden), in the lower one a very old pair of big black scales, with heavy weights. We didn't use these very much and I rather think they came into effect more in earlier days when flour was stacked in the same way. The warehouses had a dusty, wooden smell and I used to linger in there sometimes just to feel the atmosphere. It seemed to me a kind of long-ago, intensely quiet atmosphere. I would climb the stairs and stand at the top, where the window overlooked the garden and beyond and watch the shafts of sunbeams drifting across the warehouse and penetrating into the corners. There was a feeling of stillness, of waiting for something to happen that never did. We never, ever, played in either of the warehouses. They belonged to the shop and that was not the playing domain.

Tagged on to the bottom warehouse was the outside toilet, which invariably became iced up in the cold Dunstable winters. Diagonally across from that and marking the end of the yard was the coal barn. In front of that, by the corrugated iron fence (later galvanised) stood our two dustbins, which were of great use to me, as will be seen.

The garden was a boy's paradise. It was lovely, large and had lots of secret corners. A pattern existed, but it did not appear to have one. There were wild parts that were left to be wild but which nevertheless merged with the flower beds and rockeries and paths and lawns. It was tended with much enjoyment by both mother and father, on Thursday afternoons and on light evenings. But both of them just liked to walk around it and often my father would say, when we were indoors, 'I'm just going for a walk round the garden'.

From that garden came some of my very earliest memories and from that garden came the pleasure that I have had in the four gardens that my wife and I have had and made. I have no intention of describing it in detail. I could never do it justice. I can see it in my own eyes, as clearly as if it were yesterday. It is a memory made up of many things.

Of a red may tree rich in blossom, behind the coal barn; of lilacs – pale mauve, deep mauve and white – and the fragrance of their flowers in the house when mother used to pick a bunch and put them in a deep vase; of the silver birch, which every now and again would have its leaves stripped in a matter of days by the caterpillars of the buff-tip moth; of the curving, main path that led from the yard to the sheds at the back of the garden, and which bordered what we called the small lawn, the main sitting and playing area and where the washing was hung

One part of the garden, with a wooden arch on the right from which my swing used to hang in early days. The path by the small lawn went down past the side of the sheds through the low wooden gate to the bonfire and 'clearing-up' area. The little rock and stone bird-bath was the smaller of our two baths, both made by my father.

In the garden, on the curving path by the small lawn, with my mother and father. The skipping rope, I think, had been handed down and it wasn't used much.

The rhubarb was enormous . . . taken on our big lawn right round the back side of the house. The other side of the fence was the Grovers' tennis court, hence the tall wire netting.

The summer house in the corner of the small lawn, where we had so much fun. It was a family meeting-place and much used. The enjoyment we had from it must have richly rewarded my parents. Behind the summer house were the sheds.

on dry days; of the five-sided wooden summer-house tucked in the corner of that lawn which my parents had had built as a silver wedding present to themselves and where dark purple clematis climbed up the lattice work; of roses red, yellow and white; of the old rambler roses creeping along rustic framework – the little pink clusters of Dorothy Perkins and the creamy coloured larger blooms of Emily Grey; of the path bordering the long rose bed and 'the wood' and the swing constructed over that path; of the see-saw made out of a long plank and cement poured inside an old cheese drum; of the oval shaped bird bath and the rock pedestal in it with an upturned dustbin lid on top filled with drinking water for the birds; of the winding, curving crazy paving path past the small apple tree and the big apple tree; of the wild place at the end, with its bracken bed; of the 'beech tree and the Austrian pine, in juxtaposition their arms entwine'; of the wooden seat built by my father, made up entirely of rustic and on which I used to stand and watch the tennis being played over the fence; of 'snowball' trees where I used to gently crush a bloom in my hand on hot days and hold it to my face; of the flowering currant and the hanging pink blossoms that came in the Spring, with its earthy smell; of Solomon's Seal; of white and yellow jasmine, trailing along a fence; of Sweet Williams and bright marigolds and snap-dragons and rosebay and pale mauve periwinkle and sweet-smelling lily-of-the-valley, hiding in secret places, and the intense blue of forget-me-nots and speedwell; of the sunken garden, with the paved base and the little pedestal in the middle; of the sand-stone rockery; of clumps of saxifrage and bright yellow stone-crop and aubretia; of primroses and cowslips and violets – the pale mauve wood violets, the dark purple and a few white ones; of sweeps of London Pride; of white Japanese anemonies and intriguing bright orange Chinese lanterns; of the blackberry trained along the bottom fence and of laurels; of the holly; of ivy; of long sticks of pale red rhubarb with great big leaves that I could pick in season and hide behind; of the big lawn, where the garden ran behind the tall, solid wall of the house and warehouse to the back of the lock-up shop and down a side path to the gate on to the High Street; of berberis and cotoneaster; of dark blue flag iris; of variegated grasses; of rock roses; of tall foxgloves, where bumble-bees lurked; of Rose of Sharon and the looked-for Christmas roses; of 'Creeping Jenny' and 'Rachael and Jacob'; of hearts ease pansies and violas – oh, of a thousand different things . . . Spring, Summer, Autumn, Winter.

Because my sister was that much older, I was really an only child, as far as a playmate was concerned. By the time I knew who she was she was at school, first at Moreton House in West Street, a big ivy clad house with gardens, between Matthew Street and Victoria Street, then at The Cedars, Leighton Buzzard. For that journey she walked down to the lower station to catch the train early in the morning or caught a bus outside the shop. After that, it was daily work in London.

So I grew up with hours and hours in which to play by myself. Certainly there would be a friend invited to tea from time to time and sometimes to play, but early on I was very much on my own.

Two things played an important part in those years. One was a form of transport, the other a ball. Initially I was lucky to have the most splendid pedal car. It was painted purple, with black mudguards and trimmings and cherry red wheel hubs on grey tyres. There was a mock windscreen, the driving wheel was black and it had one of those old horns such that when the bulbous end was pressed a magnificent 'parp' ensued. I pedalled that car at a furious rate up the yard, down the main path by the side of the small lawn and the rose bed, up to the sheds and round and back again, yanking it round when I reached the back door of the shop. Sometimes I shot off elsewhere, but that was the main route.

The cat was the chief danger, but to itself. It had a habit of coming out of doors or up a side path at the wrong moment. It managed to escape by the proverbial skin, except once, when it really did get caught up. Eventually it extricated itself and shot off, screaming, to the nether regions of the garden.

After the motor car came a scooter, a green wooden one, but with thin rubber tyres. I used it, but it was somewhat of an anti-climax after the driving of the purple monster. Then came the regulation fairy cycle which I rode with the same abandon as I had driven the car, but which was more manoeuverable over a greater area of the garden. I did fall into the roses one day, which I found a sharp experience, but the mishaps that did occur were on my own two feet, by falling over when I was running too quickly, to the continual detriment of my knees and shins.

I must have been fourteen before I had a proper bike, but then I accompanied my father up the road to Charlie Cole's emporium and was bought a proper Raleigh bicycle with a light blue trade mark on the front, but with no 3-speed, for £4. 7s. 6d. That was what could be afforded and I accepted it with pride and joy.

The motor-car and the scooter and the bicycles, including the shop bike that the errand boy used, were kept in the sheds that I have mentioned which were at the end of one area of the garden. Also our deck chairs and all our garden equipment and tools, which included a push and pull mower and a heavy roller. This again father had made by cementing inside one of the old cheese drums. I know it had a wonky handle and was rather heavy to push, but I enjoyed rolling the lawns and was quite happy to do it.

They were big sheds, not the tiny garden shed type, and one of them was really storage space for the overflow items for the shop such as blocks of whiting, certain bottles and vinegar barrels. Vinegar didn't

The shop bike, my sister in the saddle, my father looking on and the goods in the basket. In the garden again.

Obviously the proud possessor of a brand new fairy cycle. One of the many bandages that bound up my wounds appears on my left leg.

THE motor car, Registration no. LB 2376.
I am fully aware that there will be a number of readers who, when they look at this picture, will burst into uncontrollable laughter. When they have finally wiped away the tears, I would only remind them that each and everyone of us has early childhood snaps that are as equally embarrassing . . . It would appear, from my well-cut, thick driving coat, my character headgear, my gloves and my resigned expression that I am about to leave the garden and take the Great North Road on a long-distance expedition. I only hope the spare petrol tank is full.

come in small bottles to be purchased as such. It came in a barrel very similar to a beer barrel. There was a red seal to break and a plug with a little wooden tap to be inserted which was turned to measure out the amount required into a tin mug. These barrels smelt and therefore only one at a time was rolled down to the shop area, where it stood outside the back door, under the lean-to roof.

Between these sheds and the back fence was an open area which was our bonfire place and it was generally the errand boy's duty once a week to clear up all the refuse and old boxes that could be burned. Along the fence also were the remains of a chicken run, as when my family first came to Dunstable they had had some hens. On one particular after-noon the errand boy succeeded in setting fire to this old chicken run, with its wooden top and ends. There was probably as much smoke as fire, but there was a danger to the sheds, so the fire brigade had to be called. Fortunately the fire engine was housed in the Town Hall yard, not all that far away and as the firemen were able to get round to the lane at the back as well as through the garden all was very quickly under control. Not before, however, my mother had had severe palpitations of the heart. She was walking home along the High Street with me when the fire engine went past, bell clanging. That bit of the action was fine, but not when she realised from the not-too-distant view that it had

The Borough of Dunstable's Tilling Stevens fire engine that leapt to the rescue of the Bourne's sheds. This particular vehicle was described as a 'light motor Fire Engine, with extension ladder, capacity 150 gallons per minute, with 25 h.p. Engine; solid tyres and disc wheels, purchased in 1925'. [GH

stopped outside the shop and firemen could be seen dashing around. . . .

So we come to ball games. I played these endlessly, as a lone boy, making up all sorts of games. I had been blessed – and I thank God for it – with good health, a quick eye and a reasonable talent for a moving ball. Anticipation and quick reaction came with the games I played. There was, of course, the continual game of throwing a ball against a wall – the side wall of the outside toilet, the back wall of the shop under the lean-to, the huge wall of the big lawn – and catching it, trapping it, stopping it, kicking it back. But mostly catching it and as I grew in strength and stature, so the ball was thrown harder and at angles made more difficult on purpose, in order to catch the rebound. On the big wall a tennis racquet could be used, but the main purpose of the game was simply to catch the ball and see how many times running that could be done.

However, from about the age of eight, the yard was also my domain for a ball. This yard was made up of small, oblong grey tiles, except near the kitchen door and where it met the wooden flap that lay over the outside entrance to the cellar. It stretched the whole length of the house and building and was about three yards wide. There was half the distance width again of earth, along the fence that lay between our property and next door. Apart from a few ferns, not much was grown in this except it was the place where the jasmine stretched along the top of the fence and came out in white cascades in winter, and where the Solomon's Seal was planted. I only mention this because the Solomon's Seal fascinated me, with the long green stalks and the hanging creamy-white pendulum flowers on a drooping stem. The Solomon's Seal plants that we have in our garden to-day are the self-same plants, having survived three moves between us. If I had to lose every single flower in the garden, those Solomon's Seal would be the last to go.

This yard was my football pitch. There was a natural goal at each end – the opening to the lean-to at the back of the shop, and the gap between the outside toilet entrance and the corner of the coal barn. I had to avoid a couple of sinks and be careful of the cellar flap, plus a small lilac opposite, but I could play the ball off the wall and the brick end face of the dining room bay. If the ball went into the recess of the hall porch it was a throw-in, as also if it ended up on the earth. There were no corner kicks. What I was not allowed to do, under strict orders, was to get soil all over the yard, so I had to keep the ball on the yard surface to kick it. That did not mean, however, that the fence was free from being hit.

My father had been born in Kent, so had both his parents. Likewise both sets of grand-parents and fore-bears. So I was brought up, when I began to know what cricket and football were about, to support Kent

Cleaning the fairy cycle on the cellar flap in the yard, my football domain. At the end of the yard is one of my 'goals', the lean-to covering at the back of the shop. The dining room bay window juts out just before it.

County Cricket Club. He also worked at and lived in the close association of Woolwich Arsenal. There was only one football team, therefore, that I could possibly follow – Arsenal. In the early days when my father and mother were both living in Plumstead, the team was called Woolwich Arsenal and they played at The Manor Field, Plumstead, which ground was at the bottom of mother's garden, before she was married. Mother's father also was an engraver at the Arsenal so mother therefore came into this as well and there was no doubt about it at all – Arsenal was *the* team, as they were of course not only in Great Britain but across the world.

So it was Arsenal in winter and Kent in summer. Whether it would have remained that way if Arsenal had been languishing near the foot of the Third Division (South) and Kent instead of Northants had been propping up the County Championship I do not know, but growing up in my impressionable years both Arsenal and Kent, right through the thirties, had very fine elevens, arguably the best ever in their respective histories.

When I listened to the cricket scores over the wireless in those summer evenings Kent always seemed to be scoring runs, as they were in fact, and 'Tich' Freeman was always taking wickets. There was the Kent score, 300 or 400 plus, with a century from the incomparable Frank Woolley or W. H. Ashdown or Arthur Fagg or the dashing Bryan Valentine or Leslie Todd or C. H. Knott. Or Leslie Ames.

Leslie Ames, the great Kent and England wicket keeper-batsman, was my cricket idol. But if he was the summer idol, Cliff Bastin was my football one – the Arsenal left-winger, 'Boy' Bastin, who had won every honour in the game by the time he was nineteen. It is incredible to think now, that he once scored 33 goals in one season entirely from the left wing, which must be on a par with 'Tich' Freeman taking 304 wickets in a season (many of them st. Ames b Freeman, of course).

So in my football games in the yard, played mainly with an old tennis ball dashing up and down, back and forth, doubling, passing, going into tackles, taking free kicks and penalties, scoring goals, I was nearly always Arsenal, wearing in imagination the famous red shirt with its white collar and cuffs and the white shorts. Just for a change sometimes, I was England, but then the team consisted of its share of Arsenal players and always Cliff Bastin was prominent.

Arsenal always won, although sometimes in a particularly difficult Cup-tie away from home, they drew and won the replay at home. Sometimes they won handsomely and then goals would be crashed in from all angles by Ted Drake, occasionally hitting the back shop door with a bang, which did not always go down well. Joe Hulme would chip in with a goal here and there, as did the immaculate David Jack or, very occasionally, the tiny Alex James, with his long shorts and sleek, black hair, centrally parted. But more often than not, in the matches that really mattered, in the match that decided the League Championship, or the semi-final of the Cup, or the final itself – played against the outstanding teams of the day, Sheffield Wednesday, Sunderland, Derby County, Newcastle United – it was Cliff Bastin who scored the winning goal in the final, dying minute of the game. It was his goal that brought the crowd to their feet, the trophy back to Highbury. Often my shooting was not as good as it should have been and then the referee mysteriously added on extra seconds until I did manage to get the ball in the corner of the goal (it had to be in the corner, one straight at the goalkeeper in the middle would not do) before blowing his whistle.

But as with all boys, the ball would go over the fence into next door's property. Not very often when I was smaller but as I grew more robust and more exuberant at the game I was playing, at fairly regular intervals, both at football or other games (which included being bowled at by a friend with empty biscuit tins as a wicket – they made a great noise when they fell over, as can be imagined). The ball over the fence is where the dustbins came in handy. I could stand on these and if I wasn't able to see the actual ball, at least I could make a very good guess – the judgement improved with the passing of time – where it should be. Then I would lift myself up, jump down the other side, find the ball, hopefully quickly and clamber back over again. This, of course, could only be done by the blind eye, the acceptance of the principle, the good-will, kindness and general understanding of our neighbours.

Fortunately for me there had been a change of scene next door. I had never liked going round via our sideway and their sideway to ask Mrs.Gravestock 'if I could have my ball back, please'. It was not fully appreciated. But after a few years the 'hat-shop' closed, Mr. Wilcox the hairdresser came for a short space of time, renting the shop, and then the original neighbours moved.

Which is where the Sewells enter the scene. Mr. David Sewell, the fishmonger, the last of the character tradesmen of our High Street North, and his good lady. Mr. Sewell came from Billericay in Essex and was proud of it, although he had been in Luton, on and off, for some years. But he came to Dunstable and rented a fish and chip shop in Ashton Street, not to be confused with Ashton Road opposite the shop.This was the small street that ran along the back of the properties of Middle Row in High Street South. It was bordered by small terraced cottages, 'The Eight Bells' on the corner of St. Mary's Street, the public lavatories and more small houses to the edge of West Street. Ashton Street was also known as Back Street and all this area spreading backwards in rows of houses, cross streets, three pubs, and the 'Institute' in Chapel Walk, as far as Bull Pond Lane, is now Ashton Square and the sprawl of Sainsbury's and the big car park. Only the old Baptist Chapel remains.

There was no proper fishmonger's in the High Street at our end of the town. Mr. Sewell remedied this by buying no. 129 and setting up one of those delightful fish shops that every town worth its name used to have. It was a real fishmongers in the same way as my father's shop was a real grocery. Open to the pavement it sold some thirty different kinds of fish, all laid out for the customer to see on marble slabs. Shrimps were sold by a half-pint measure and packets of bread crumbs were sold from a little office in the corner. It had dark green shutters which were pulled down at closing time by a long pole with a hook at the end.

Mr. Sewell was a well-built man, small of stature, but with a big heart and he fitted into the community of High Street North exceedingly well. My parents were very pleased to have Mr. & Mrs. Sewell next door and it also meant they could now buy fresh fish with the minimum of effort. The shops also complemented each other and the two families were very happy neighbours, with a friendship that carried on long after retirement years.

The Sewells did not always enjoy peace and quietness, when I was going full pelt in the yard. Apart from the normal noise of kicking a ball about I used to keep up a running commentary on the football match I was playing and when the winning goal went in I sometimes used to leap up in the air and shout "GOAL – BASTIN!" at the top of my voice, such was the exuberance of the moment. Regrettably, on one particular

Having established his shop at our end of the town, in March 1937 Mr. David Sewell opened another fishmonger's in Middle Row, opposite Moore's. This photograph, in which it was suggested to the populace that they would be healthy if they ate herrings, was taken on the first day of opening, Mr. Sewell standing proudly by the side of the counter on the left. The shop took over the site of The Countryside Library, which existed for a brief spell, but before that it was where Hooton's Bazaar traded, mentioned in the next chapter. [DS

occasion Mrs. Sewell was just coming out of her back door when this noise split the air. She was so startled that she dropped the plates she was carrying, which smashed to pieces. I did not know of this, she said absolutely nothing to me or my parents, and I only heard about it, from Mrs. Sewell herself, much later in life.

They had a baby daughter, whom I regret to say I woke up from time to time. However, this little girl, at a tender age, was awakened by thunder in the night and called out. Her father went in to comfort her only to be greeted by the words "Is it that naughty Colin, again?".

So Mr. & Mrs. Sewell appreciated my situation as an only child, they had an understanding of what a ball over the fence meant to a boy and how lost he would be without it. Thus, they helped, in that understanding, to my undoubted enjoyment and welfare.

Chapter 4

'TO TALK OF MANY THINGS'

Home and garden, house and street, the town itself.But there were certain individuals that flitted in and out of the home scene in Dunstable or items that were part of the town itself. There were events that happened each year or were one-offs. . . .

. . . the man who came round, before the fish shop opened, with shrimps on a tin tray, and a tin mug for a measure. Father nearly always bought a mugful, so that day we had shrimps for tea, whisking off the outer shell and cracking the head.
. . . the muffin man, tray on his head, ringing a large bell.
. . . the Indian travelling salesman, with a coloured turban, a long overcoat and an outsized suit-case that he seemed to have some difficulty in carrying. He appeared twice a year, calling at houses, knocking on doors.
. . . the knife-grinder, with his pedal cycle and box and his cry of "Knives to Grind". He would stop by the kerb and turn his wheel and the knives would come back, sharp as new.
. . . the cry of the rag and bone man, standing up on his flat cart, pulled by a clattering horse.
. . . the lamp-lighter, going round at dusk with a long pole, to switch on the gas lamps, inside their glass covers. In the main street there were lamp-posts, sometimes in the back streets the lamps were on a bracket attached to a convenient wall.
. . . Percy Ashwell taking his hat off to a lady. Percy Ashwell had a haberdashery in High Street South, his shop door being where the entrance to Gibbs & Dandy is now. He was also a Funeral Director, so he was a well-known Dunstable personality. Those were the days that if a gentleman was wearing a hat, or a schoolboy his cap, you automatically took it off if you passed a lady acquaintance. In the same way, a seat was always given up to a lady in a crowded bus, you always stood up if a lady entered the room and the man always walked on the outside of

a lady when accompanying her on the pavement. A lady was a lady and was treated so. It was generally agreed in Dunstable that nobody could take his hat off to a lady like Percy Ashwell could. There was all the graciousness and flourish of the Elizabethan era, all the courtesy of the Victorian era, all the ceremony of the Edwardian era in his one single gesture. He was a much respected man, was Mr. Ashwell and much admired, naturally, by the ladies of the town, even if they did not say so.

. . . the Corporation steam-roller, one of those all-powerful looking, massive machines, with its glinting brass, hissing steam from its engine as it rolled the newly-laid surface on the road, guided and looked after by one man who must have been the Prince of all drivers.

. . . and the tar machine, with its big cauldron and tongues of fire, the long-handled shovel worked by sweating men and, above all, the pungent smell.

. . . the thick fogs of November, the snow and ice of December and January, the cloudbursts in the summer that the drains could not cope with – great lakes across the High Street opposite 'The Sugar Loaf' and down our way, the water tumbling down Union Street, and below both bridges.

. . . the week of the Boat Race. I would go across to Mr. Parsons and buy my light blue favour to wear on my shirt or coat. Cambridge also dominated the thirties. I knew which crew to support alright.

. . . Cup Final Day, when there was a team, or teams, from the north playing, which was nearly always the case. The coaches would start coming through at an early hour of the morning for Wembley, the first one around eight o'clock and reaching a climax, one after the other, between ten and eleven. Scarves would flutter out of the windows, men sporting big rosettes sat inside and it was all a good-humoured affair, out for the day with a smile on their faces (at least, going there).

. . . in a similar vein, the red-letter day when Arsenal were drawn to play at Luton in the 3rd round of the Cup, early in 1934. Mother made me a beautiful small red and white rosette, father somehow managed to get away from the shop, which he was rarely able to do, and off we went, to sit at the end of that draughty old stand, with its wooden benches, at Kenilworth Road, to watch *the* team. To actually see them! They didn't let us down.

. . . Laurel and Hardy at the pictures, 'The House of Rothschild' with George Arliss, Charles Laughton in 'Mutiny on the Bounty', Wallace Beery, Joe E. Brown, 'The Invisible Man', Tarzan, Eddie Cantor, Charlie Chan, Shirley Temple.

. . . the fête in the gardens of Grove House with the Dunstable Excelsior Silver Prize Band playing away, Mr. Dolman conducting.

. . . garden parties at Dr. Lathbury's house ('The Limes') in West Street, through an old gateway, just above the old Frances Ashton

6th May, 1936, floods in Dunstable! A huge hail-storm blocked all the storm gulleys. Luton was untouched. This photograph shows High Street South, looking towards The Square and the end buildings of Middle Row, with the spire of The Methodist Church predominating. The first vehicle casualty is the Stop Me and Buy One tricycle of Wall's ice-cream. On the left, near the last tree, are the permanent posts and poles of the cattle market that was held weekly, each Wednesday. The Teas Hovis sign on the right belongs to Mr. Boxford, the baker, and further down there are signs advertising 'The Saracen's Head', which public house knows all about being flooded, down through the years . . .

[P.C.(DS)

The long-distance coaches lined up in High Street North, near the old Town Hall. It was on the balcony of this building that all the election results, borough and national, were announced by the Mayor to the waiting crowd below.   *[LM*

Almshouses. Also in Dr. Pargeter's garden at 'Montpelier House' in High Street South.

. . . the express coaches that used to stop at Dunstable en route from London to the Midlands and the North and vice versa. They would pull up one after the other in the High Street between the old Town Hall and Albion Street and there was often time for the tea rooms of the Central Café (painted orange with black trim) and the 'Whipsiderry' next door (yellow paint) to do a roaring trade. A few people got on them at Dunstable, too, to go north, and tickets could be bought in advance from Eddie Hunt or from Mr. Franklin's shop, near the Borough Gazette office and next to the green and yellow facade of the Liberal Club, which had its own premises and was a reminder that in the past Dunstable was a strong Liberal area. I would often watch the coaches go by, at the appointed hour of the morning – Standerwick, Scout, Midland Red, Yelloway, Majestic. . . . they were the successors, really, of the old stage coaches and Dunstable was continuing its history as a staging post.

. . . the day when the R101 airship went over the lower part of the town, down by the railway bridge.

. . . orange-rolling on Good Friday afternoon on the Downs, when it

A photograph of the Statty Fair taken in 1947, but roll away the years and the view was virtually the same. This also is a late afternoon picture, before the lights fully came on and lent enchantment and excitement to the scene. Behind this section of the fair, which often started with a boxing booth on the corner of Friars Walk and went right along to stalls in Ashton Street, are the old Transport Dining Rooms (here belonging to Picton, but in earlier years, Hicks) and, next to the church, the Central Corn Stores that once belonged to the Farmborough family and then became Bunkers. That interesting building disappeared to make way for the entrance to the present day car park.

[DG(GG)

was a regular custom and properly done. I didn't go every year, it depended on 'the order of the day' at home, but I went a few times and was part of a large army of boys (were there some girls there? I suppose so, but I didn't notice them) on the very lower slopes of Pascombe Pit. That is where we stayed, the oranges were *rolled* down the slope as custom demanded and we scrambled for them when they reached us or sometimes got stuck a part of the way down. There was never any throwing of the fruit, nobody charged up the slope and nobody got hurt. There was a way to do it, it was done and everybody enjoyed themselves.

. . . the Statty Fair that took place on the last Monday in September, a kaleidoscope of colour and noise that spread along the whole face of The Square from one end to the other, one of my red-letter days of the year. The power and tradition of this Fair, decreed by ancient statute, was that long, long after they had gone there as children themselves, and then taken their own children, elderly citizens of Dunstable would

Silver Jubilee Day, 6th May, 1935. A section of the carnival procession proceeding along High Street North towards the cross-roads. 'Way in the distance can just be seen the water tower at the top of High Street South – then a much more predominant landmark than it is to-day.   [SJ]

TO TALK OF MANY THINGS'

wander down to The Square on the night of 'The Statty' and just stand on the other side of the road and watch and reflect.

. . . a meeting of the Literary Society in the Town Hall, packed with 400 people. For several years father was on the council. I was allowed to go occasionally and sat on a hard chair right at the back of the hall, legs jumping with half-cramp. Mother was asked to take the chair once and accepted, which was a brave thing for her to do, in front of all those people, as she was a reserved person, really. Once we entertained the speaker for the night – Captain Knight of Golden Eagle fame. He was a leading ornithologist of the time and I remember him having breakfast with us the next morning.

. . . the Silver Jubilee of King George V and Queen Mary in May, 1935. The town en fête with flags. We had a big Union Jack and two smaller ones on yellow sticks flying from the front of the house. Father decorated the shop windows in red, white and blue. On the day itself there were events all over the town and a very big carnival procession. Two years later, at the Coronation of George VI and Queen Elizabeth there were street parties everywhere, including one in George Street, and each child was given a commemorative mug.

. . . the evening when one of the glider pilots was up over the Downs, trying to break the endurance record. It was given out over the wireless in one of the news bulletins and when it was dark some people took their cars up to the top slopes and parked, headlights full on, to light the scene and give support to the pilot.

. . . the arrival of the Michelin man in the town, one afternoon. The Michelin man was really an advertisement for Michelin tyres and he was completely covered in white tyres of various sizes, the largest, not surprisingly, round his middle. It so happened that I was with my mother, approaching Scott's garage in High Street South and homeward bound when this apparition more or less fell off a lorry and lurched along the pavement. As his face couldn't be seen it was really quite frightening and I wasn't at all sure of what was happening. It was, of course, an appropriate place for him to be, outside Messrs. Scott's large establishment of sales room and garage, with its big double name-board, A.A. and R.A.C. signs and pumps that sold ROP, National Benzole, Red Line and other petrols, as it was not only a landmark in High Street South but in Dunstable itself. Scott's, which commenced trade in 1882, was opposite The Square, next to Priory House and very close to 'The Saracen's Head' and I suspect that motorists filled up at both establishments.

. . . three postal deliveries each day, early morning, mid-day and mid-afternoon, the postman coming into the shop with the mail. My father would post a letter to Luton in the pillar box near the corner of George Street early in the morning before the first collection and receive a reply

The showrooms of Scott's Garage, 1931, fronting High Street South. There was also a big workshop, a car park and lock-up garages. [CS

the same day by the afternoon post. The General Post Office was open every day of the week from eight o'clock in the morning to seven-thirty at night, plus Sunday morning for an hour and a half, nine to ten-thirty, for postal purposes. Service to the public was the maxim.

. . . exploring the cemetery for the grave of A. O. Jones, England cricket captain against Australia in 1907–08 and captain of Notts. In a career of just over twenty years (he died early, aged 46), he scored nearly 23,000 runs with 34 centuries and was regarded as one of the finest fieldsmen ever to grace a cricket ground. Apart from this record he has one other claim to fame and a permanent niche in the game's history. It was A. O. Jones who invented the gully position. His gravestone was erected by Nottinghamshire County Cricket Club 'In Memory of a great cricketer'.

. . . walking down Nicholas Lane, off High Street North, between Charlie Allcorn's premises (Halfords now replaces that old facia) and 'The White Hart'. Fifty yards down the lane was a blacksmith's. Then there were railings, behind which was an orchard and two tennis courts where members of 'The Hawthorns' club played. Then came Dunstable Town Bowling Club, with its compact green and its attractive pavilion. Father was a member and sometimes I would go down with him, in the holidays. The President was a tall, very civil, upright person by the name of Mr. Mann and the Cheshire family (father and three sons) were

Mr. Fred England's double-decker 'XL' bus, a photograph taken just before delivery in December 1931. A Dennis, it was a 50-seater and became the pride of the fleet. Because of its work load and its serviceability, it came to be known as 'Bashing Kate' by those who worked it. [RB

much in evidence. The Bowling Club and the tennis courts were a restful oasis in the middle of Dunstable and could also be approached by a path between houses off Church Street, somewhere around 'Kingsbury Court' and Ashton School. All of this is now swallowed up by The Quadrant shopping centre and the car park and development behind the school.

. . . walking up the rough track of Sleepers Lane and Buttercup Lane, now Canesworde Road, along hedgerows drenched with may blossom and Queen Anne's Lace, to the edge of the golf course and then round by the farm. The way near the golf course was past a big dell where wisps of pale blue harebells trembled in late summer.

. . . Mr. Bright's single-decker bus, which used to operate a service from the bus stop in West Street to Eaton Bray and Edlesborough, and back again. Also an early memory – Mr. England's big blue 'XL' double-decker that lumbered along the main highway with a service to and from Luton via Houghton Regis. Then later his 'Union Jack' and 'Bluebird' services.

. . . Hooton's Bazaar, one of the character shops of Dunstable until it was knocked out by the advent of Woolworths in the mid-thirties. Situated in Middle Row, a few doors down from The Square, alongside the Singer Sewing Machine shop and next-door-but-one to Mr. E. J. Buckle's gentleman's outfitters, it was also known as The Penny Bazaar

Hooton's Bazaar in Middle Row around 1928. It was one of a chain of such shops and in this picture socks and handkerchiefs can be seen displayed, with a row of small toys and dolls hanging below. The girl in the centre was a Miss Phyllis Clarke, seconded from the St. Albans Hooton's to be manageress of the Dunstable shop. Miss Clarke lodged in Dunstable for the week and went home at the week-end. But she married a Dunstable man and became Mrs. Sydney Bird. She is now in her eighties after over fifty-five years of married life and still lives in the town. [SB

and many of the items were only 1d or 2d. The goods were displayed on the left of the shop in continuous long, sloping divisions and customers walked in at the right which was open to the elements. A shutter was pulled down at night. It was a real bazaar, selling all kinds of items from kitchen utensils and darning wools to gaily coloured trinkets and bangles. And toys, which is why I liked shooting in there if I had half a chance, to look at the farm animals and the soldiers and the games.

. . . the two-minute silence each year at eleven o'clock on the eleventh day of November, to remember those fallen in the Great War. Everything and everybody stopped. Buses, lorries, cars, pulled in to the kerb and switched off their engines. People got off bicycles, reined in their horses. Everyone stood still. Nothing happened in the shops, in the houses. There was an utter silence, everywhere. It was only when I grew up that I realised how close the Great War must still have been to our parents.

The Royal Silver Jubilee of 1935 gave an opportunity for the whole country to celebrate – after all it was the first one for 73 years. Celebrate it did and Dunstable was no exception. In fact Dunstable really 'went to town'. A whole series of events, planned by an executive committee set up under the chairmanship of the Mayor and assisted by an enthusiastic number of citizens, took place from seven o'clock in the morning to midnight. Big crowds attended these events on a dry, sunlit, early May day when "No one was forgotten; everyone was provided with ample facilities for enjoyment. It was a day the like of which Dunstable has never before known; may never know again".

The day started at 7 a.m. with 'Joy Peals' from the Priory Church. At 10.30 a Royal Salute of 21 guns by the Battery of the Bedfordshire Yeomanry Territorial Unit. At 11 a Divine Service on the Recreation Ground. At 1 p.m. a Luncheon for 200 old people in the Town Hall. At 2 p.m. Children's Sports on the Recreation Ground, for girls and boys aged between 7 and 14. 160 children, all organised beforehand, took part in Flat Races, Egg and Spoon Races, Shoe Races, Skipping Races, Sack Races, Treacle Tin Races (?) and Obstacle Races.

After the day, Waterlow & Sons, whose management and personnel helped considerably to its success, produced a detailed 48-page Souvenir booklet, incorporating a number of photographs taken by the staff of Home Counties Newspapers and including extracts from the Dunstable Borough Gazette of 8th May. The two pages that follow describe the events from the Children's Tea at 4.30 p.m. onwards.

CHILDREN AT TEA.—First Drinks from Jubilee Mugs.—After the sports the children were marshalled into four groups, and headed by bands they marched to various halls in the town, where a sumptuous tea awaited them. Beside each child's plate was a special commemorative mug, which he or she afterwards took home. A host of willing helpers made light work of the serving of the meal, and soon each child was enjoying a tea long to be remembered.

During the meal the Mayor looked in at each of the halls to assure himself that the children were enjoying themselves.

The teas were served to the 1,300 children at the following halls : the Britain-street scholars at the Methodist Church, the Square : the Chiltern-road scholars at the Town Hall ; Ashton Boys' and Ashton Girls' scholars at Messrs. Waterlow's Concert Hall ; and the Burr-street scholars at the Victoria-street Methodist Hall.

FIELD DEMONSTRATION.—Territorials in Action.—The most pacifist of people cannot help being interested when confronted with the activities of soldiers. There is something about the swinging step of a column of infantrymen that quickens the pulse, while the sight of big guns is calculated to invoke a feeling of awed curiosity in almost everyone, from the smallest of small boys to the oldest of ardent pacifists.

Thus the field demonstration by the 419th Field Battery R.A. (T.A.) Beds. Yeomanry, presented on the AC-Sphinx Sports Ground, held its own in popularity with any item on the Jubilee Day programme.

At the conclusion of the display, the Battery advanced in formation towards a dais, which had been erected at the Dunstable end of the field. The prizes were presented by Brig-Gen. R. N. Smyth, who congratulated the Battery and the winners on their efficiency.

A PROCESSION OF SPLENDOUR.

A MILE OF TABLEAUX

Brilliant Spectacle on Parade.

Of all the events of Dunstable's wonderful day of celebration, the one item that will remain in the memory after the rest are forgotten—if, indeed, any item of Silver Jubilee Day is forgotten—will be the great carnival procession, about a mile in length and including some sixty massive mounted tableaux, which paraded Dunstable's main streets and made the town impassable to other traffic for nearly two hours.

It constituted an amazing example of the ingenuity and craftsmanship of the Dunstable artisan. A dozen tableaux descriptive of the British Isles and the Empire followed the Mayor and members of the Town Council, who walked over the whole long route with the Excelsior Band at their head, and behind came a wide variety of subjects, on wheel and on foot, mingling humour with pathos, history with the present and, perhaps, the future.

"As good as the Lord Mayor's Show," was the description of not one, but dozens of the spectators who were qualified to draw a comparison, and they spoke with sincerity.

The task of judging this magnificent array assembled in Great Northern-road, Priory-road, and Station-road, was a colossal one, particularly as the exhibits were of almost uniform excellence, so that the adjudicators were deserving of sympathy, equally as much as those entrants who received no tangible reward for their labours.

The organiser was Mr. W. G. Thompson, who is worthy of sincere congratulation upon the unprecedented success which attended his efforts, and Mr. E. Dutton was chief marshal.

The various sections were under the marshalship of Councillors H. H. Todd and L. Gibbons, Mr. S. E. Farbon and Mr. C. Dutton, and when the judging had been completed were quickly on their triumphant way past the densely lined pavements, while other spectators, from the vantage points of windows, were particularly favoured, despite the fact that nearly every window frame was crowded with heads. The route taken by the procession was along High-street South, West-street, and Chiltern-road, returning to High-street and the Square, where Mrs. V. E. Goodman distributed the prizes.

THE FIREWORK DISPLAY.—Thousands Enjoy Brilliant Spectacle. —The largest crowd of the day was undoubtedly that at the firework display, held in the grounds of Park Farm. It is not easy to estimate the number of people in a crowd, but there must have been at least five or six thousand. The field allotted for the display was packed, and as there was only one exit it took a considerable time for the crowd to disperse when the display was over.

PORTRAIT IN FIRE.—But popular as the preceding programmes had been, it was the finale which evoked the most enthusiasm. This took the form of a portrait of the King in twinkling points of fire, flanked by the inscription "1910—1935." While the crowds were applauding this, races of rockets and salvoes of shells brought the display to a conclusion.

Thus ended what was, next to the procession, the most spectacular event in a day of spectacle, and the crowd slowly surged forward towards the narrow gate and the next item on the programme.

LIGHTING THE BEACON.—Scouts' Torchlight Procession.—At the conclusion of the firework display a large section of the crowd made a trek for the Downs to watch the interesting ceremony of the lighting of the beacon.

Scouts marched to the Downs bearing lighted torches, and on their arrival at the beacon, which had been set up at the highest point above Pascombe Pit, they formed a circle of light, which the Mayor entered and called for three cheers for the King.

THE FINAL SCENES.—Tableau on Town Hall Balcony.—And so came the end of this most memorable of days. By a quarter to twelve a crowd some thousands strong had gathered outside the darkened Town Hall for the Mayor's remarks, and the final tableau which was to mark the end of one of the most eventful and spectacular days in the history of the borough.

Punctually at a quarter to twelve the Town Hall lights were switched on, and the flood lighting apparatus, which had been turned off for a short period, again brought into use. The Mayor in his robes of office, and accompanied by the Mayoress and members of the Town Council and Jubilee Committee, stepped on to the balcony to deliver his address.

"LOVE, LOYALTY AND DEVOTION."—" This day," he said, " will go down as a great day in the history of the borough. It has been a great day because of the spirit of love, loyalty and devotion which has been shown by my fellow townspeople towards their gracious Majesties King George and Queen Mary."

He wished to place on record his real and sincere appreciation of the splendid work put in by every member of the local committee. No one could have wished for a more loyal body of workers.

" Much more could be said, and ought to be said," concluded Ald. Cook, " but time is short, so please accept my very real and sincere thanks. You have done magnificently, and great are the thanks due to you."

THE FINAL TABLEAU.—The address over, the lights were again extinguished until a few minutes before midnight and the final tableau.

The effect of the scene was added to by a spotlight focussed on the central figure in the tableau, a young lady dressed in white, and carrying a bouquet of lilies, representing Peace, and standing in front of Britannia.

But probably the most impressive moment of the whole scene was when someone on the balcony invited the crowd to join in singing the last verse of "Abide with me". The hallowed words were taken up by a thousand voices, and given added meaning by the whole-hearted unison of the singing.

As the last strains died away, midnight struck ; there was silence for a moment, and then the band began the National Anthem, the crowd stood to attention, and with great fervour words that were in the hearts of everyone were sung.

As the National Anthem ended, there was again silence for a moment or two, and then the great crowd seemed to spring into animation, and cheer after cheer was raised. Gradually they dispersed. Jubilee Day was over.

THE MAYOR'S THANKS.
"We were excelled by none."

Dear Mr. Editor,

Will you please allow me, through your columns, to emphasise what I have said elsewhere, namely, that I feel greatly indebted to each one of my fellow townspeople who have played any part whatever in the wonderful success of the Jubilee celebrations.

Sir, it would be an impossible task to enumerate the names one by one, because so many have volunteered to help, and offers have come from the large works in our town and their staffs, and from every organisation in the town.

Therefore, Mr. Editor, I would like to assure your readers that there is no one more gratified than myself for all the sacrifice and work put in to make our Jubilee celebrations such a great success, and I think I can rightly claim that, for a town of its size and the number of its inhabitants, we have been equalled by few and excelled by none in our splendid loyalty and devotion to the Royal Family.

With real and sincere thanks,

Yours sincerely,
ALFRED COOK, Mayor.

[SJ

Chapter 5

SUNDAYS AND 'THE SQUARE'

Sunday, at home, was a day of rest. It was a different day, a day set aside for quiet relaxation, of being together as a family, of enjoying the fireside in winter and the garden in summer. And of going to church. For my parents the hard work of the week was past and this was the day to reflect and give thanks. It was the Sabbath and it was kept so.

Looking back on those Sundays, they were lovely days, really, and I wouldn't complain about them in any way. There were certain things I was told not to do, there were certain matters I was expected to do and I accepted both as perfectly justifiable. It was the way of life for that day of the week and I wouldn't have thought of doing otherwise. Not at that age, anyway.

I wasn't allowed to play any ball games on a Sunday, so the neighbours also had a peaceful day. I could play games, of course, but they were to be quiet ones and I was encouraged to read one of my annuals or an adventure book. Sometimes a jigsaw was at hand and that would be done. There was no gardening done on Sundays and the lawns were never cut then, even if it had been wet in the week and the grass needed attention. (Now I come to think about it I don't remember any one else round about cutting their grass, either). The garden on a Sunday was there to enjoy peacefully, to walk around and to sit in. The odd weed might be pulled up in passing, but that was all.

Likewise, indoors, there was no housework done. There were, of course, meals to prepare and mother, bless her, would make sure that we were well and truly fed and that the meals would be something special, befitting the day of the week. Breakfast had none of the usual coming and going, so it was boiled eggs, the one day of the week where there was variation. Sunday lunch, the peak meal of the week, was all prepared and mainly put in the oven before we went to church and heaven help any minister who preached too long and caused anxiety to rise in the minds of the ladies of the church. It didn't often happen but there were occasions, particularly with a visiting preacher, when his zeal over-rode his common sense. Mother would begin to fidget (that made two of us), sidelong glances would occur and when the service was over, there were wan smiles of greeting all round to friends and then we would shoot off home, mother muttering dire warnings of retribution to the Lord's emissary if her beautiful roast joint was burnt. Very occasionally the Superintendent Minister of the church, or his number two from Toddington, would go over the accepted limit. If that happened the Society Steward would politely say to him afterwards "Bit long this morning, Super, don't you think?" If he was wise the minister would inwardly digest the hint. After all, he had to face his own wife when he got home, as well.

Tea-time, on a Sunday, was special, too, whether it was round the fire in the dining room (never in the living room) or out in the summer-house or on the small lawn. Apart from the normal fare there would be scones and a new home-made cake, baked the night before, and either a tin of fruit, or a blancmange, or a jelly, or sometimes a combination of them. Or one of mother's delectable trifles. Aside from meals, mother would often read and there was nearly always a letter for her to write. There was no Sunday newspaper and in fact my parents never took one right to the end of their lives. Bearing in mind the size of a Sunday paper today and the gloom and doom it often portends that was really quite a sensible idea.

In the winter, certainly, and sometimes on other Sundays as well, there was always a special treat for me in the afternoon, in that I was allowed to look into my father's tin of foreign stamps and, as I began to start a collection of my own, to choose a certain number. At first they were common ones that I was allowed, then as I began to understand stamps a little more and appreciate the differences, so the choice was widened. My father and his twin brother, apart from their interest in butterflies and moths, had also collected stamps. They had hit on the idea of writing to post-masters of all the countries in the British Empire, plus a few foreign countries, explaining in their letter that they were keen young philatelists and hoping that they might be able to send them any stamps that might come their way. They had had some very satisfactory replies (I suspect partly because they said they were girls) and by this method and all sorts of other ways they gathered together quite a wide ranging collection, enough certainly to whet a small boy's appetite when opening the old Oxo tins full of them. My father hadn't put his in an album, whilst Uncle Charlie had (it was father that had mounted the butterflies and looked after those), so that really made it all the more exciting for me, delving into the pile.

So these couple of hours on a Sunday afternoon, fortified by a twopenny bar of Cadbury's milk chocolate from the shop (another treat) were great enjoyment. It wasn't long before I started my own album, a very simple one at first. In time I decided I would concentrate on the British Empire and leave on one side the South American countries and the old German states and the Espanas and the Belgiques of this world.

From the beginning I had my favourites. I would drool over the multi-coloured stamps from Zanzibar, with the Sultan's head in the centre; the kangaroos of Australia; the ships of the Turks and Caicos Islands; the camels of the Sudan; the pictorial ones of historic scenes that came from Canada. I also had a great affection for our own classically designed stamps, including the monarch's head above the denomination and the differing colours of Hong Kong and Mauritius and the Gold Coast and Ceylon and the Straits Settlements . . . and so on.

Stamp-collecting (philately was too strong a word for a boy collecting stamps) also gave me one big advantage by the time I went to the Grammar School. By then I had a considerable knowledge of where countries were all over the world, as well as some of the states within those countries which once had issued stamps of their own, such as those in Australia, and Natal, Orange Free State, Transvaal, Zululand etc. in South Africa. Then I tried writing overseas to Old Boys that appeared in O.D.'s notes at the back of the school magazine and even had a go at the 'letters to Post-Masters' idea (but as a boy). The former, I remember, brought in a super mint set of Kenya, Uganda and Tanganyika and the latter two pen-friends. One was the son of a sponge merchant of Greek extraction in the Bahamas and the other, in complete contrast, a middle-aged lady in Antigua. Both were on a stamp exchange basis and this correspondence went on for a number of years. Many, many years later I was in St. John's, Antigua, briefly, on business. I enquired about this lady. It turned out she had been very well-known throughout the island, was a much-loved and respected character and had had a wonderful stamp collection. I like to think that just a few of mine had helped make that collection.

It would seem, from my deviation into the world of stamps, that I have strayed again from the basic text (an applicable word, perhaps) of this chapter, although that deviation was a result of childhood happenings on a Sunday. But whatever we did or did not do on the seventh day of the week, going to church, for my parents, was of the utmost importance and Sunday really revolved round attendance at morning and evening services. Mother and father had a strong faith and apart from the fact that they both felt that it was the right and proper thing to do, they went to church because they wanted to thank God for all their blessings and to take their part in an act of worship in God's own house; they could relax completely in the atmosphere, it was very meaningful for them and they sang the hymns with enjoyment and prayed quietly with reverence. They took an active part in the affairs of the church.

I was taken, in the same way as my sister, who became a member of the choir in her late'teens, had been taken and I soon accepted that fact. Church on Sunday, twice, and going to some of the lighter week-day events, was a considerable part of my early life and I was fortunate once more in that the church to which I went and in which I grew up was a big, handsome church which a lot of families with children my age attended; it was a church of character with many characters as members and it also played a considerable part in the life of Dunstable. No doubt to a large extent due to the care given me at home, I felt comfortable in that church and in the fullness of time, in a quiet way, responded to the atmosphere.

The Methodist Church on The Square was (and is) a dominant building in the centre of the town. (So also had been the previous chapel, burnt down one September night in 1908 in one of the biggest and most devastating fires the town has ever witnessed). There were a large number of inhabitants in the town and in the villages around who were practising Methodists or of Methodist extraction, the greater majority being Wesleyan. Many of the tradesmen of the town attended the church. It had a very large Sunday School, two big Bible Classes and the Church itself had a capacity of over 950, filled to overflowing a number of times at special services each year. It had had a day-school in the halls at the back and there was also the old Institute building up

The ruins of the second chapel on the site, which had held 1300 people. Just fourteen months after the disastrous fire, in the first week of December 1909, the new building – the present church – was opened and the first service was held.　　　　*/MC*

Chapel Walk, opposite the side gates. There were also sixteen chapels scattered around the villages that made up the circuit. With all this and the regular and special events that took place all the time in the church and in the various halls that made up the large suite of buildings, it had an effect on Dunstable which was fully recorded in the pages of the Dunstable Borough Gazette, both in writing and in photographs.

In spite of the beauty and the solid strength of the Priory Church, with all its history and the good congregations that were also enjoyed there, Dunstable really was a non-conformist area, with the three Methodist Chapels, the two Baptists, a large Congregational building in Edward Street and a small Mission Hall called the King Street Mission, plus of course, the Salvation Army. Thus it was natural that the church on The Square would be very much a central point of attention. It was a Wesleyan Methodist Church until union with the Primitive Methodist Church came in 1932. There are still people in Dunstable who, to-day, refer to it as 'The Wesleyan Chapel'.

After union and up to the war years (and indeed beyond) it was known as The Square Methodist Church, in order to differentiate it from the church in Victoria Street. However there were so many wits around the town that wanted to know why Methodists were square and what did a square Methodist look like, anyway, plus those innocent folk who genuinely thought that The Square Methodists was another branch of non-conformism, that the title was gradually turned round to The Methodist Church, The Square.

I am told that there were three of us christened one Sunday morning early in 1925. Me and two baby girls. Or to put it more politely, two little girls and myself, all three of us children of tradesmen. I don't know in what order we were christened. I suspect the two little girls were 'done' first so as to soften the impact of the blow that was to follow. On the other hand the thorn might have been put in the middle of the two roses, so as to better the impact that way.

What I do know is that all three infants grew up to play a part in the church in which they were christened. One of the little girls moved away with her family at a fairly early age of her childhood, only to return later to marry the brother of the other little girl. This second girl stayed around locally a long while, plus work in one of Europe's tiny principalaties before moving away to get married. The piggy in the middle (or the one at the end) has lived all his life in Dunstable, save around eight years. He was also the best man at the marriage mentioned above.

After the period of the Dog Kennel walks, I went to the morning service and then was taken out by my father during the hymn before the sermon, a very sensible decision if I might say so now. Disruption of the sermon by me would not have gone down very well. Once I distinctly remember being taken out promptly well before the sermon, as I would neither, on that particular Sunday morning, keep still or quiet. "Are we going home, now, Daddy?", I said in a loud voice.

Then came staying through the whole morning service, sermon and all. It was, of course, the sermon at the end of the service that was the trying part, the long-drawn out part where there was no singing or reading or bowing of heads, or even the taking of the collection, which was quite enjoyable to watch. The sermon could be anything between twenty minutes and half-an-hour (mercifully this latter timing no longer exists) and the best part of it was when the minister closed the big pulpit bible that was in front of him. That was the signal that he was coming to an end, only a couple of minutes or so remained and I would stop digging father in the ribs to ask my perpetual question of "How much longer?". I felt very cheated indeed when the minister, occasionally, went on much longer than I thought he should have done after closing the bible. That was not playing the game.

At that age mother stayed at home with me in the evening whilst father went again. I would watch father put on his grey spats and his immaculate grey homburg hat and then take his walking stick. It was always best clothes for going to church and a very high standard was set by all who attended. That generation would not have thought any other way and generally speaking so do their sons and daughters.

Evening service came along for me, as well, as soon as I was thought old enough, so we all walked up together, except for my sister who, being in the choir, would go a few minutes earlier. (I was never expected to go to Sunday School, so I was spared the 'three-deckers' that some of the children had when they had grown up a bit). After a while evening service presented no particular problem for me as I sorted out one or two mental games for myself, which I tried to keep for the sermon. Counting the organ pipes (43) in varying sequences was one. Another was counting up the three columns of the hymn board, where the numbers of the hymns were displayed, to see which column had won. This had to be done line by line and then added to, rather than total each column up one by one, so it took a certain amount of mental arithmetic and stopping and starting again. Then there was the game with the same hymn board where the proper sequence of numbers had to touch one another to proceed. Thus if 0 touched a 1, then I could hope that 1 would touch a 2 and so on. I reckon a whole chapter could be written on pastimes people play during a sermon. . . .

The evening six o'clock service at that time had a larger congregation than the morning at 10.45, though both were well attended. Now it is completely the other way round, even more so. During the course of the year there were two evening services at least when the church was packed out – Sunday School Anniversary and Harvest Festival. I remember for the latter that if we wanted to sit in the pew in which we

75

normally sat we had to leave home before half-past five to be certain of that place. I also remember extra chairs having to be placed in each aisle as well (in a church of downstairs, gallery and choir stalls of over 950 seats, mark you), such was the attendance. To join in the harvest hymns, with a full organ going and everybody singing in a packed church, was a wonderful experience, even for a small child.

Harvest Festival, the third Sunday in September, was an outstanding day for me. Apart from the hymns with their captivating tunes, the church was magnificently decorated with flowers and fruits and harvest symbols. The whole length and depth of the inside of the altar rail was a great splash of colour, with produce given from members of the church from all over the place. For many years mother was one of a small group of ladies whose responsibility was to ensure that the decorations for Harvest matched the festive day. Produce would come in on the Saturday morning and early afternoon, the flowers would be stood in buckets and jugs of water, and work commenced around half-past two. It would be completed around six or seven and then, to the satisfaction of all concerned they would stand back and look at the finished display. Yes, it was good enough. Yes, it would pass judgement.

In the centre was generally the harvest loaf, specially baked by Mr. Boxford, and flanked by sheaves of corn. Bunches of purple and green grapes dangled tantalisingly from the pulpit. Great bunches of mauve, purple and wine-coloured michaelmas daisies vied with long stalks of golden rod, bright dahlias, asters and zinnias, tall bull-rushes brought in from the country by Mr. & Mrs. Percy Flemons, chrysanthemums, sprigs of cotoneaster with red berries (looped along behind the pulpit),a big vase full of carnations, the last gathering of sweet peas and roses, different-hued gladioli.

People saved their prize possessions for the Harvest. It wasn't a case of "What have we got for the Harvest?" It was "Don't pick that or don't pull those up – they're for the Festival". So there were brought a huge marrow, scrubbed potatoes and long, tapering carrots. Turnips and parsnips; tomatoes. Baskets and baskets of polished green and red apples, some of which were put out in rows on appropriate perches. Plums and damsons. A few jars of home-made preserves would come – lemon curd, jams, pickles, crab-apple jelly, chutney. Eggs placed in wicker containers. A lump of coal and a glass of water would be placed on the altar table.

The whole was embellished with swathes of greenery – laurel, ivy, privet, old man's beard which would also be tied around the gallery and up the pillars. On the side window shelves would be placed small vases of flowers and there would be a display on the table in the vestibule, to be seen as people came up the wide steps into the church.

It was all a lovely display of gratitude, symbolising in full one of the great yearly anniversaries of the church and after the morning service many of the congregation would go to the front and look at the beauty of the gathering together of flowers and fruit from field and garden. I was entranced by it, sometimes helping in a small way on the Saturday afternoon and I know how pleased my mother was at the end of that Saturday when she felt that all the hard work and all the generous giving had been accomplished for yet another year and the beauty of the church itself had once again been enhanced.

(My helping was generally by way of filling vases, pots, etc. with water and carrying the produce in when required from the Choir Vestry. One year, with a friend, the 'help' was to endeavour to place a row of alternate green and red apples in an almost inaccessible place, i.e. the ledge in front of the organ pipes and to tie the contoneaster to the panel which shielded the organist in such a way that a couple of sprigs would tickle the back of the organist's neck. In both cases we were successful – the latter only momentarily – but a repeat performance the following year was not allowed to get off the ground.)

After the evening service all the children's gifts brought in at the Sunday morning service were taken out for the poor and needy and sick, and then on the Monday evening came the Harvest Sale and Supper. The produce was auctioned off amidst great enjoyment and competition before we sat down to the supper in the School Hall at long trestle tables, covered in white rolls of cloth. It was a happy time, Harvest Festival, and there were many people who used to go from one place of worship to another for their Harvest Festival services, they were enjoyed so much.

Allied with Bible stories, first at home and then in some of the lessons read aloud, it was really the hymns that led me, gradually, into the understanding of going to church and to an understanding of the Christian faith. It has been said that Methodists were known for three things – hymn singing, faith teas and prayer meetings. I know nothing of the last because we never went to any and there was no desire so to do; prayers when you went to bed at night and prayers in Church on a Sunday were sufficient, at least in our estimation, although, of course, I accept that many people have received help from such meetings.

Faith teas I knew a-plenty, as I went to enough of them with my mother in particular, but also with both my parents. Mother used to serve with a group of ladies called The Church Working Guild, which did a tremendous amount for the church. One of the major items of this group was the organisation of teas and suppers and making and obtaining enough food for them, all of it generously given. They were good teas, they were, and those people sitting near me made sure I had my share of the cakes.

But it was the hymn singing that was notable and that in turn

A corner of Mr. Durrant's main showroom in his High Street North shop.   *[DD*

depended a great deal on the organist. Mr. Will Durrant was the first organist that I can remember – a quiet, true gentleman who was a cabinet maker and upholsterer and had a bright, airy furniture store in High Street North, next to the Sugar Loaf Hotel. He was a fine, thoughtful organist, but in my formative years the organist that I remember so much and whom I enjoyed so much was Leslie Boskett. He was at the organ right through the thirties and in fact until the late fifties.

Mr. Boskett used the full range of the organ, every key, every note, every pedal and he played the instrument to the requirements of the hymn and the words of the hymn. If the hymn talked about a still, small voice, then there was a still, small voice on the organ. If the trumpet sounded, then there was a trumpet sound. If the golden evening brightened in the west, then the organ played as though there was a golden evening brightening in the west. And if there was a storm at sea, then there was a storm at sea, right there in the choir stalls. To sing, for example, 'For all the Saints', 'Eternal Father', 'There's a light upon the mountains', 'My heart is resting, O my God', or even 'All things bright and beautiful' with Leslie Boskett playing the organ was a revelation and the combination of beautiful words, memorable tunes and the organ played as it was, started me out on the right road, at least.

At the end of the twenties there had been enough boys who were interested to have a few in the choir, for the morning service, which was unusual for a Methodist church. For two or three years, therefore, when I was about ten or eleven, I became a choir boy for a period and of all the unlikely events that occurred in my early life, looking back, I reckon that was one of the unlikeliest. Not that we were dressed in white surplices, of course, there was nothing like that, we just turned up in our best jacket and short trousers. It was the voice since those days that makes the event so difficult to comprehend. However, it did happen and for those months I was in the front row very close to the organ, so I really could appreciate all the more Mr. Boskett's performances.

I could write about hymns in the Methodist hymn book for a long time, because over the years they have meant so much to me, at times of joy and at times of sorrow, at good times and at difficult times. But I mustn't get carried away too much. Sufficient to say that I think there are those hymns that have some of the loveliest poetry ever written and some of the most outstanding lines. How do you surpass, in its context

> . . . 'And so the shadows fall apart,
> And so the west winds play;
> And all the windows of my heart
> I open to the day'

or the lines 'Where cross the crowded ways of life' or 'For the mystic harmony linking sense to sound and sight' or 'Pavilioned in splendour and girded with praise', or the verse

> 'Drop Thy still dews of quietness,
> Till all our strivings cease;
> Take from our souls the strain and stress,
> And let our ordered lives confess
> The beauty of Thy peace'

or, finally, the verse from the harvest hymn that is so evocative of England, the seasons and the goodness that we have been given:

> 'In the spring the smiling meadows
>   Donned their robes of living green,
> As the sunshine chased the shadows
>   Swiftly o'er the changing scene;
> In the summer-time the story
>   Of a riper hope was told;
> Then the rich autumnal glory
>   Decked the fields in cloth of gold'

Of course there were dirges with lines that were very difficult to understand. One of these started 'O God, Thou bottomless abyss'. I could never ever understand why God was a bottomless abyss. There were also those whose rhyming left a lot to be desired, including one or two very prominent hymn-writers. It went against my awakening literary interest to have to sing lines that rhymed 'have' with 'gave' and 'lamb' with 'same'. So they were frowned upon. It also caused me great amusement, when I found out that both previous chapels had been burnt down, that the congregation sang with great gusto and with not a flicker of an eyelid 'See how great a flame aspires' and 'O Thou who camest from above, The pure celestial fire to impart'.

Although I can recall one earlier minister, there were really two Superintendent Ministers that spanned my memory of those years and both of them were characters. Rev. George Brewin came in 1931 and had a large family. His youngest son was my age, so I came to know the inside of The Manse in Great Northern Road fairly well. (Later on I came to know it for another, much more interesting reason). Mr. Brewin was a strict disciplinarian and ruled the youngest son with the proverbial rod, but he was a good minister, very active, and worked hard all round the circuit with the support of his very motherly wife. He had a motor-bike and could be seen charging out to the various village chapels and communities that came within his jurisdiction.

The second minister who came in 1934 was entirely different, save for his work-load and again with family support. Rev. Francis Gatehouse was a man of the classics, yet was happy to talk to the smallest child and the humblest labourer. (You may say, "Well, so he should" but there have been parsons in all walks of the Church who were not prepared so to do). He had a goatee beard, stained with nicotine from his cigarette smoking, a large hawk-nose and piercing eyes. He had a great sense of humour and was a scratch golfer. He was caring, affectionate and very friendly, in spite of his, to a child, awesome appearance. All his family entered into the life of the church and all of them are remembered where others have long since been forgotten.

I can recall an ending to one of his sermons. He shut the pulpit bible with a thud, leant on it, looked at the congregation and said "And I wonder what the angels thought of that". I've no doubt the angels welcomed Francis Gatehouse in the course of time. He left for another circuit in the late summer of 1939 and his successor, Rev. Wilfred Lawson, a quiet, respected gentleman, had the mortification on his first service in his new church of telling the congregation that War had been declared.

It is interesting to note that these ministers and all their predecessors and all the special visiting preachers that we had on such Sundays as Harvest Festival, the School Anniversary, Church Anniversary, Wesley Guild Anniversary and so on all had to make themselves heard from the pulpit, in this big church, with no microphone or any artificial aid to

Week-day evenings at the church were nearly always a hive of activity and there were many enjoyable social occasions. This picture is of a mock Lord Mayor's Banquet in 1937 arranged by the Wesley Guild. On the stage of the school-hall at the 'Lord Mayor's' table, left to right: Ray Moore, Harold Kenworthy, Rev. Francis Gatehouse, Horace Darby, Mrs. Darby, Mrs. Gatehouse and Fred Moore. [FTM

help them. A major part of their training was elocution and the ability to throw their voice, so that no-one would miss the message they had to convey. I don't remember any problem arising in that matter.

As in many Dunstable organisations, a number of the members at the church on The Square were characters and personalities. Most of them were well-known in the town, being tradesmen. Some of them took part in civic affairs and held the highest office of Mayor of Dunstable, at a time when that meant the Chairmanship of the Bench as well. Some of them became Aldermen, as well as Councillors. Some were J.P.'s. These Dunstable folk led very busy lives during the week, yet they still took the time to serve their church on a Sunday, as well as often acting as a Trustee for 'The Square' and one or two of the smaller places. A number of them were local preachers and with their colleagues in the villages took services all over the circuit, often in bad weather, particularly in the snows of winter. With a circuit of 17 chapels, 31 pulpits had to be filled on any Sunday. The two ministers, one in Dunstable, one in Toddington, would only be able to take six services at the most,

METHODIST CHURCH,

THE SQUARE, - **DUNSTABLE.**

Sunday School Anniversary

PALM SUNDAY, APRIL 5th, 1936.

Preacher :

Rev. Francis B. Hudson

of Wolverton.

Services - Morning 10.45   Evening 6.0

In the Afternoon at 2.30

A SPECIAL YOUNG PEOPLE'S SERVICE

to be conducted by Scholars

Speaker : Rev. F. B. HUDSON.

On Monday, April 6th,

A PUBLIC MEETING

Will be held in the Church at 7.30 p.m.

Scholars and Teachers will present a Play, entitled

"BOYS and GIRLS OF THE BIBLE."

Chairman : Mr. M. S Lockhart.

Special Singing by the Children and Choir at all Services

Organist - Mr. Leslie Boskett, B.Sc. L.T.C.L.

Collections for School Funds

Enterprise Works, Dunstable·

The cover of a booklet for the Sunday School Anniversary services on Palm Sunday 1936, showing the special visiting preacher. Rev. Hudson later became the Superintendent Minister of the Dunstable circuit, after several years in Bedford. He had one special attribute – a smashing daughter, who later became my wife. Inside the booklet are fourteen pages giving all the hymns that were to be sung, with the names of the young soloists at the top of the relevant verses. On the back cover was printed the Balance Sheet for 1935 for the Sunday School. The income side included Anniversary collections of £43.17s.1d and sale of sweets £3.18s.6d. Expenditure included £2.9s.0d for tuning pianos and £16.2s.1d for Prizes, Magazines, Equipment. Balance in Hand was £1.14s.0d.   *[MC*

assuming an afternoon service could be included. Two or three might be taken by a Supernumerary Minister (retired) living in the area, but generally speaking there were around 25 pulpits to be occupied in scattered villages, ranging from Hudnall and Dagnall in one direction to Greenfield and Westoning in the other and including also Houghton Regis and Leagrave. That this was achieved, Sunday after Sunday, speaks very highly of these men.

There were, of course, too, the offices of the church to be filled, this often involving mid-week meetings. My father was not a local preacher, it was not his forte, but over the years he was a Poor Steward, a Society Steward, a Circuit Steward, Secretary to the Trustees and a Trustee himself, plus any special events that came along that might need a Secretary or a Treasurer or his help somewhere. So one way and another I came to know some of the grown-ups of the congregation.......

Joseph Flemons and his family used to sweep down the left-hand aisle to sit in the transept Sunday after Sunday, wet or fine. This Flemons was the Flemons of the recently departed Flemons & Marchant and he had a small herbal factory just off High Street North, down a lane called White Hart Lane. This building could also be reached by a cross path from Nicholas Lane. Percy Flemons was the son that took over from him and many of the children of the neighbourhood used to go out into the fields and country and bring in quantities of dandelions, wild mint, rose hips, fruit of blackthorn, tansy and such like for the herbalist. (Even poppy heads, but that did not mean that Mr. Flemons had an opium den tucked away). They would then get paid a penny or twopence a bagful according to the quantity and the value thereof.

F. J. Creak was a dapper little man who owned a hat factory in Luton (Currant & Creak) and sat in the back centre pew with his family. He was always smartly dressed, with a wing collar, spats, a buttonhole and a cane with a silver knob. He had a large house very close to The Manse in Great Northern Road and he would walk briskly down the street, looking all about him all the time. From around the middle of July and through August the Creaks would disappear from Dunstable and retreat to a bungalow they owned at Trevone, near Padstow. As far as I know no-one else in the church had a similar hide-away and we thought it was something very grand to be able to do that. Mr Creak was Mayor of Dunstable 1923–24 and gave much service to the town. His greeting to me was a jovial kind of "Good morning, young man, how are you to-day?".

Amos Gray followed Mr. Creak as Mayor. He lived in Priory Road and was another one who sat near the back of the church. He was in hats, too. He was as slow and deliberate in his walk as Mr. Creak was quick and nimble, being a much larger man. He seemed to me to look at small boys with a rather whimsical look, as if to wonder why they should exist at all. Both Mr. Gray and Mr. Creak were Governors of the Grammar School.

Alfred Cook (or Alf Cook as he was always known) was Mayor of Dunstable for no less than four years, from 1932 to 1936, so that his service to the town can never be doubted. At the corner of Britain Street, where the shops lie back, he was a dealer in new and second-hand furniture at the rear of his store and a greengrocer in the front, a curious combination. A tall person, Alf Cook had a shock of white hair and moved around at great speed (I suppose you had to if you were Mayor for that length of time). In spite of having to address hundreds of meetings, open dozens of bazaars or the like, give scores of after-dinner speeches, etc. his voice was not all that easy to follow and I regret to say that there were those, myself included, who were rather inclined to imitate him. But there was no doubting his sincerity about his love for Dunstable and for 'The Royal and Ancient Borough', which phrase he often used right at the beginning of any remarks.

The person who followed Alf Cook as Mayor of the town, in Coronation year, was yet another Methodist and one with whom I came into contact a good deal, as I was friendly with two of his children. Frank Kenworthy had been stationed in Houghton Regis in his Army days in the First World War, from his native Yorkshire. He met his future wife at the church and after the war he decided to make his home in Dunstable. For the rest of his life he lived here. He was a striking man, with a prominent jaw, blunt but kind and had an unswerving loyalty to his church and a dedication to any task or office he undertook. He was a local preacher of note, often taking the morning service at 'The Square' and he and his family took an active part in many church affairs, all of them holding office one way or another. Mr. Kenworthy was a baker, initially, in High Street South and then later opened a furniture store in West Street, not far from the cross roads.

It is strange that all of us can remember a trivial incident, an insignificant item that occurred many, many years previously, whatever it might be. A traveller can remember a fleeting scene out of the window of a train, a sportsman one shot or stroke, a gardener a single flower. I can recall, clearly as anything, one sermon from Mr. Kenworthy in which he kept on talking about *obstackles*. The fact that I can remember anything at all about a sermon is surprising enough, but Mr. Kenworthy did have a riveting voice and this word *obstackle* kept on coming out, over and over. I had no idea what he was talking about. It turned out to be his Yorkshire pronunciation for obstacle. . . .

There is a good story told about Frank Kenworthy and another baker, Herbert Boxford, who was also a member of our church. New families moving to the town were not numerous in those days and anyone coming in was courted by the tradesmen for their trade. There was no waiting to let events take their course. On this particular occasion there had been new people in Priory Road, about half-way along. It so happened, by sheer coincidence, that Mr. Kenworthy and Mr. Boxford turned the corner of Priory Road from two different directions at exactly the same time, both intent on visiting the new lady of the household. After a dozen steps or so they recognised one another from afar and realised the situation. Each one tried to quicken his step without the other one knowing. Then quicker and quicker until in rather an unseemly scramble they both reached the gate of the house in question together. Unfortunately and with much regret I do not know who won, if either of them did, that is. I don't think, being Methodists, they would have tossed up, not in that day and age. But if one of them did turn out to be a winner, my money would have been on Frank Kenworthy.

There used to be big iron gates at the entrance to Grove House gardens, when the house ceased to be a private residence and the gardens were opened early in 1939 as 'Public Pleasure Grounds', which were given to the town in memory of Mrs. Kenworthy, the Mayoress, who died not long after her husband was Mayor. They were fine gates, with her initials on them, but alas they are no longer there, having been replaced with a rather inferior-looking set. There is a small plaque,

The memorial gates that were erected as an entrance to Grove House gardens. The Borough arms can be seen over the centre span. [*GH*

however, on one of the side pillars referring to the gift – and stating that they were opened by the Rt. Hon. Lord Luke of Pavenham, Lord Lieutenant of Bedfordshire.

I have mentioned four Mayors of Dunstable. There were two other former Mayors in the congregation at the same time that I am talking about, but to be honest I didn't really know them and therefore I cannot justifiably talk about them. Equally so it would be unjust not to mention them in the context of high civic office and church life. W. E. Seamons was Mayor in 1920–21, Joseph Andrews in 1922–23. Mr. Seamons was a nurseryman in West Street, Mr. Andrews was a baker and confectioner in High Street South, next to the old International Stores. He, too, was a local preacher. So from 1921 to 1937 there were six Methodist mayors, totalling nine years of service.

To add to the story, Mr. F. G. Keep, who was a member of the Victoria Street church, was Mayor for three years in 1937–40, so this service also must be taken into account. Mr. Keep kept (!) a newsagents and sweet shop at the corner of Middle Row and West Street for many years and that corner of the cross roads is still referred to by elderly Dunstable folk as Keep's Corner.

And to add a further point of interest, all these mayors and their colleagues in those years took office on November 9th each year, to tie up with the City of London.

Mr. Percy Lester was a jeweller in Middle Row and was recognised as *the* jeweller of the town. For many years he and his very pleasant, caring wife lived over the shop, where the floors and walls, being a very old building, were not always level. The name of Lester will be remembered for a long time in the annals of the church as there were two distinct branches of the name and they were very long-serving. It still seems extraordinary to me that in two pictures on the same page in the book 'Old Dunstable', compiled by Bill Twaddle, (first published in 1975 and recently re-issued) of the Methodist Church trustees in 1909 and 1950, Mr. Lester is in both of them, standing at the back on the right. Percy Lester was a very quiet man, extremely sincere, and both he and his good lady did a lot for the church in their own quiet way. They had no family, which was a pity, because they were very tolerant of children and showed affection to them. They were very good friends of my parents and sometimes we would be invited to supper after the evening service. Mr. Lester had a habit of nodding off every now and again and on one occasion he fell asleep at the top of the table whilst we were eating.

Charles Moore was an upright, tall man who looked and was a pillar of the church, dedicated in every way and ensuring, with his wife, that his four sons were also brought up in the same manner. With his white hair and carefully trimmed moustache and his slow walk he was a

W. E. Seamons 1920–21

Joseph Andrews 1922–23

Amos Gray 1924–25

F. J. Creak 1923–24

The
METHODIST
MAYORS

Alfred Cook 1932–36

Frank Kenworthy 1936–37

F. G. Keep 1937–40

[OR

87

striking figure. In earlier years he had the draper's shop next to Charlie Smy in High Street North, but had moved to High Street South, where the shop still exists, now greatly enlarged and under the control of his eldest son. In High Street South the shop was between that of Mr. Andrews and James Tibbett, fancy goods and printer (the early beginnings of Index Printers) and member of another well-known Dunstable family. Mr. Tibbett then sold out to Boots. Softly spoken, Charles Moore was very strong on attendance at Sunday School, as well as at church itself. He was also a local preacher, so was his father and so was his grandfather. And in turn so were his sons. The Moore link with the church and the town has been kept alive all through the years and recently the shop celebrated its 80th anniversary in business, one of the very few real family shops left in Dunstable.

A. J. (Joe) Parkins was a haulage contractor – a removal man. It was said that if you had an awkward piano to move in an awkward place, then send for Joe Parkins. Honest as the day in his everyday business, like all these people I have mentioned, he served his Lord seven days a week in everything he did. A local preacher all round the area, he was much respected and furthermore much loved. He was of medium height, very wiry (no doubt from his job), a kind and happy man and with a loud singing voice that he used for every line of every hymn whether he knew the tune or not. I know because he occupied the corner seat in front of us. Joe was one of four brothers, one of whom went out from Dunstable to be a minister, whilst the other two lived elsewhere. But Joe was *our* Mr. Parkins and I cannot think of him as being anything else than a permanent fixture at the church.

Mrs. Will Durrant (the wife of the organist previously mentioned) was one of the most faithful members, a quietly spoken, quietly moving, pleasant lady who lived well into her nineties and had an indomitable spirit and, as it turned out, reserve of strength. But although I well remember her at church services and in the context of the church, there is another reason why I recall her now. Mrs. Durrant was on my mother's 'calling list' – they were good friends. So when mother went to see Mrs. Durrant in an afternoon, every now and again in my tender years, I had to go, too. The Durrants lived in a big, three-storey house on the south side of West Street, with steep steps and a climb up to the front door. We always conversed – at least my mother and Mrs. Durrant did – in their front room, a large bay-windowed room with solid furniture, ample chairs and in the décor of that age. I sat on the edge of a chair and tried not to look bored, I knew there was a saving grace. After ten minutes or so, never before and as long as I had been polite, Mrs. Durrant would look at me kindly, with a fraction of a smile and ask me if I would like a sweet. She would then go to a highly polished sideboard, on which stood a silver entrée dish with a cover. This would be lifted up to reveal a few sweets. Now with apologies to Messrs. Fox and Nuttall I cannot remember whether they were glacier mints or mintoes, but whichever they were I am grateful to them and to Mrs. Durrant, because that sweet gave me the challenge to make it last for the rest of our stay and enabled me to survive the visit.

To get back to spiritual reality. . . . J. H. Abell I have already mentioned in another context, otherwise he most certainly would have been introduced here. He gave his Sundays to Methodism. George Gadd was a little man who was a greengrocer, next to Mr. Lester's. It was one of those interesting old style greengrocer's shops, on a par with our grocery shop and Mr. Sewell's fishmongery. I knew him and his wife well, also the house, as I was in and out of it through a happy friendship with one of his sons. They had dark and spacious cellars underneath the house and it was rumoured that they were part of the so-called underground passage from the Priory into West Street. Alfred King ran the Bedfordshire Supply Co. in Church Street, a clothing store, recently taken up by a gunsmith and a lingerie boutique – I wonder what he would have thought of that? He was a staunch member of the choir and his tenor voice was heard in concerts all over the place. And 'Uncle' Melville Lockhart, that most generous, understanding and kind-hearted of men, one of the Lockharts of Dunstable. Once he took two of us to Lord's to watch Middlesex play Kent.

There are four other distant memories. The man with a patriarchal long white beard who used to sit all by himself in the front row, bang in the middle of the gallery and would exclaim 'Hallelujah' every now and again during the sermon. The upright tall man at the side of the gallery, again by himself, who was a porter at the Church Street station and a local preacher. The little man with the benign face who regularly, every evening service at five to six used to open the lower church door off the corridor at the other end of the church itself – grey suit, wing collar, buttonhole, puffs of white hair – and go and sit in the near transept. Finally, Nurse Ann, who was a fully qualified midwife and nurse and who in the week was dressed in the dress of the Crimea, sitting near the front with her companion, as the sunlight filtered through the windows and sunbeams danced round her large, grey bonnet. . .

Of course there were many others; I have named but a few, but they were persons, for one reason or another who made an impression on me. But amidst this congregation of contrasting faces, build and livelihood and with the ministers very much part of our lives, I gradually grew into the church and accepted its teaching, for which I am very grateful, although I am sure I have failed in many ways. But I have never been one for evangelical thumping of the table and crying out for conversions. I am highly suspicious of both for I suspect these lead in many instances to a more intense 'religion' that in turn can cause problems in family and national life. Yet I wish more people would accept the part and the place that a church can play in their everyday lives. They miss so much.

Methodists liked garden parties, particularly when they could sit down to tea. Our big lawn at home, with the wall of the house going up and up, was large enough to have a small garden party. This picture, taken probably in the summer of 1932, shows one such gathering on behalf of the church. Extra chairs, with wicker-work seats, were brought down from the church premises. There is also a seat, with horizontal slats, that can be seen, second down from the front. This was an old tram seat, with a moving top so that you could sit either side, and I think we acquired this from one of the old Luton trams. The little man in the front, a regular attendee at church, is Cornelius Vater, who once upon a time had a furniture store in Middle Row. His wife sits next to him. I remember him particularly for his name, which I found fascinating.

Chapter 6

CHRISTMAS

The Christmas season for us really started no earlier than three weeks before Christmas Day itself, probably nearer two weeks. There was none of this interminable planning and talking about Christmas for weeks and months ahead that goes on now and which so often can lead to a complete anti-climax.

It began really with the appearance of the boxes of Christmas crackers, the bottles of non-alcoholic wine, the decorated tea-caddies, the tins of biscuits, the special 'goodies' in the shop. Particularly the crackers which fascinated me with their gay colours and their different size boxes and the thought of the paper hats and little objects that they might contain. "I wonder which box is going to be ours?" I would think, as a small boy, little realising that mother would already have had first choice and that a box lay tucked away somewhere where little hands wouldn't find it. Often, in fact, the contents of our box had table fireworks in them, which were great fun. One I remember was a small round pellet out of which came a revolting black wriggling snake. Another was supposed to resemble the Indian rope trick.

As well as the mince pies that mother made for the shop about a week beforehand, neatly laid out on cake trays, she would also make mincemeat. This would be made in a big round earthenware bowl and the sticky contents would be ladled out with a wooden spoon on to greaseproof paper and wrapped up. Our own Christmas cake would be made about the same time and I would be called into the kitchen to help stir the appetising mixture in mother's cream-coloured bowl. Also to drop in the silver threepenny bit in the home-made Christmas pudding. Later I would watch the icing being swirled expertly on the cake and the little decoration of an Eskimo all wrapped up in white fur sitting on a white sledge placed in one position and a small robin redbreast in another.

Our Christmas cards would be bought about a fortnight beforehand

91

(they were never in the shops before December, in any case) and put in the post a week ahead of the actual day itself. We would start receiving cards sent to us no earlier than the fifteenth of the month. I was given a special spot in the room to stand up my own and it was an understanding in the home that I could open any envelopes that were addressed to "Mr. & Mrs. E. C. Bourne *and family*". We had a post on Christmas Day morning and in fact there were people who sent their cards to arrive particularly on the day itself, thus making them a real Christmas greeting.

I cannot recall Dunstable having any town Christmas tree and very few shops had individual ones. Mostly the shop decorations were strands of silver and brightly coloured tinsel and maybe a few paper chains and the odd bauble here and there. But because of the light shades of the time and the naked lights (i.e. no glaring neon strips) and the special Christmas contents added to the normal sales, the shops seemed to have more appeal then. Nearly all of them had notices in the window stating that the proprietor wished to pass on his compliments of the season and to hope that his customers would have a very Happy Christmas and a Prosperous New Year.

Outside the various greengrocers or just inside their doors would be individual Christmas trees and big bunches of mistletoe for sale, and many trees were only bought on Christmas Eve and decorated that night. Likewise the chicken or the turkey or the goose or whatever was often only purchased on the 24th. The greengrocers, too, would suddenly display flat boxes of delicious looking tangerines, many of which were individually wrapped in silver foil with here and there an occasional one covered in blue foil, thus adding even more enticement to the fruit and more sparkle and colour to the general scene.

There were a lot of carollers and the choirs of both the Priory and our own church would go out in full, down the High Street, often with a lantern on a long pole and suitably attired. The week before Christmas was all hustle and bustle, it was the only week like it and it was all geared for just the two days. On the morning after Boxing Day the shop would open at the normal time of eight o'clock and Christmas would be over. If the festive days happened to fall on a Saturday and a Sunday there were no extra days in lieu. That was just hard luck. The best break that could be achieved was when Christmas Day fell on a Friday and there was then a three-day holiday after the shop closed late on Christmas Eve. Buses and trains ran on both Christmas Day and Boxing Day, albeit not a full timetable, and thousands of people, if they had been away, had to travel home on Boxing Day evening. As a result of all this I'm sure the meaning of Christmas and the enjoyment of it was far greater than the prolonged atmosphere and unreality of to-day.

Many families have rituals at Christmas, sometimes of a general nature, but sometimes only familiar to a particular family. Our own personal, special ritual was on Christmas Eve and it took place at bedtime. It was called 'To bed, to bed, we go', and it had started, so I gathered, in my father's own home when he was a small boy.

To start off with I was put on my father's back, or as soon as I got too heavy, behind him hanging on to his coat tail. My sister would come behind me, holding on, and mother would bring up the rear. We would then proceed, father leading the way, through every room in the house, starting at the end downstairs, going up the stairs (with great care) on to the landing, round the big bedrooms, along the landing and down the step, knock on the bathroom door as we passed (much too small for all of us to get in and around), into the Rose Room and finally into my room where I was dumped on the bed. All of this was carried out whilst we sang, to a simple tune, over and over again, a little verse that had been made up by my father's elder sister, my Auntie Winnie:

> To bed, to bed, we go
> 'Tis Christmas Eve, you know,
> Hang up your stocking with right good will
> For dear old Santa Claus to fill.
> Hurrah, hurrah, hurrah!

It was one of the high spots of my Christmas time. Since then it has continued to be handed down through my sister's family and through mine and now, nearly a hundred years since it must have been written, 'To bed, to bed, we go' is still carried out each Christmas Eve and with the same excitement to our grand-children, the same wonder of anti-cipation that tomorrow is Christmas Day, that I used to feel.

Christmas and Boxing Day, for us, in the home, were spent every year with Mr. & Mrs. Pickering, our closest friends in Dunstable and in due course part of the family. Mr. Harold Pickering, well-known in Dunstable and the surrounding district and very much respected, was Surveyor and Sanitary Inspector to the old Luton Rural District Council, which included a scattering of villages around Dunstable. He and his courteous wife were both northerners and they brought to their every-day living in the town the true northern hospitality and a caring and kindness for other people. They lived in a big, rambling house at one end of West Parade, opposite the corner of the Grammar School playing field and which reflected in its contents (the pictures, the china, the antiques) the wide travelling that Mr. & Mrs. Pickering had done through Britain.

Very soon after coming to Dunstable my family had struck up the friendship with the Pickerings, thanks in the first instance to their kindness on our first Christmas in the town, and it was a friendship that was to last right through to the end of their respective lives. There were mutual interests, everybody liked one another, there were two daugh-

Late in 1931, the Dunstable Borough Gazette started a series of caricatures, each with a very pithy and racy commentary, entitled 'Among the Notables'. No. 23, in the April 27th edition of 1932, showed Mr. Harold Pickering – an extremely good likeness. Along with plans associated with his leading position in the Luton Rural District are his bowls woods. Mr. Pickering was a keen bowler, good enough to have represented the county. He held several positions over the years, including that of Hon. Secretary, in the Dunstable Town Bowling Club. [DG(EB)

ters for my sister to play with and then go to school with. Only in due course she went one better and married the son of the household, Jim Pickering, who was one of the nicest men I have ever met and a good sportsman in every sense of the word.

We simply spent Christmas together – Christmas Day, after the opening of our own presents, in the Pickerings' home, Boxing Day in ours. So there was a sharing of generous hospitality, of complete harmony and companionship, of the sheer pleasure of two eventful and happy days. Competitions and games were always a main part of the days and we never broke up until the early hours of the next morning. Charades were always played and were a particular high-spot, as were Dumb-charades, Murder, Consequences and 'Shop'. The only blot on the landscape, as far as I was concerned (apart from one competition that Mr. Pickering always had – guessing the mileage between various towns in England – which the Bournes hadn't got a clue about!) was coming out of a comfortable warm room on Boxing Day morning, about one o'clock, into the cold air of Dunstable and having to walk home through the silent streets. It had a very depressing effect on me, home seemed miles away. . . .

The Christmases of childhood are often the most nostalgic of memories. They can also bring back sad and, sometimes, not so pleasant thoughts. I can only say that Dunstable was a good place in which to spend Christmas, and family and friends at that time of the year mean more to me than at any other time.

The marriage of my sister Eileen to Jim Pickering, 18th July 1936. This delightful wedding group was photographed in our garden on a lovely, sunny summer afternoon.
From l to r standing: *John Willison (who was a very fine elocutionist, much in demand for concerts), Elizabeth Pickering, Kenneth Duncombe, Mr. Harold Pickering, George Higgs (the best man), Jim, Eileen, my father, Ken Harrison, Margaret Holt.*
Seated: *Mrs. Pickering, Edna Holton (whose father used to have a grocer's shop in St. Peter's Road), Ella Pickering, my mother. In the front, on the ground (an appropriate place), the bride's brother, in his best suit, with clean white Eton collar, white carnation buttonhole and matching pocket handkerchief . . .*

Chapter 7 (1)

SCHOOL DAYS
MISS WHITWORTH'S

I cannot really remember either of my parents saying to me that I was going to school next year, next month, next week or telling me about school. No doubt they did so, but there is no memory of my first day or any preparation for it. In those days, of course, there were no play-groups or nursery schools or pre-school activity to involve children and to get the idea of things ahead, so coming up for six years of age there was one day when before-school life ended and one day when it began.

For reasons that were not explained I didn't go to one of the council schools, but to a very small private school at number 56 Burr Street. There were three, at least, private schools in Dunstable at that time. One was Doretta Lodge in Priory Road, another was the redoubtable Misses Chambers' establishment at 'Aberfeldy', a big house near the old Post Office. I went to Miss Whitworth's. I have never heard this little school referred to then or since (and it is still remembered, though long since gone) as anything other than 'Miss Whitworth's'. For all I know it might have had a proper name like 'Miss Whitworth's School for Gentle Folk', or 'The School for Sons and Daughters of Tradesmen – Prop: Miss Whitworth'. It was not even known as Miss Whitworth's School. It was just, plainly and simply, Miss Whitworth's.

Miss Whitworth herself was very tall and incredibly thin. This was accentuated by the clothes she wore. A long tweed skirt, of some indeterminate browny colour, brown shoes, a high buttoned-up blouse with a collar, over which sometimes was a woollen jacket, again of brown or beige. Her grey hair was done up with a bun and she wore glasses that were inclined to perch at the end of her nose. She did, in fact look like a school-marm. She was fully qualified and a good teacher for the boys and girls she taught, coming to their first school. There was a proper sense of discipline, but she was also kind and considerate and I suspect, looking back, that she had the odd twinkle in the eye that was never allowed to be revealed. She did not let herself get away from the

96

image that she presented and ran a school that was highly recommended.

She was one of those women that you could never ever imagine being a small girl, running around, shouting, laughing, crying, getting up to mischief. It was quite impossible. In fact I came to the conclusion, later on, that one day God in His Infinite Wisdom created Miss Whitworth and brought her down to this small bay-windowed house in Upper Burr Street and deposited her there with the words "Now I want you to open a school here and suffer the little children yourself". So she did just that and she carried out His wonders to perform very successfully.

Miss Whitworth also went to the Priory Church, which put her on an entirely different plane. Anyone who went to the Priory was different. At the Priory they had peculiar sorts of services at odd times called by such names as 'Matins' and 'Evensong' and a funny thing called The Creed or some such that everyone stood up and mumbled, or so we were told, and which apparently they all knew by heart. They never had a straightforward Morning Service or an Evening Service, like we did. It was rumoured that they even had church services in the week, every day. I could just about follow the names that had become familiar – Wesleyan Methodists, Primitive Methodists, Waterlow Road Methodists, Baptists (I gathered they were very strict indeed and their services went on for hours), Congregationalists. Even the odd King Street Mission I could somehow incorporate into my thinking. They were all chapels. But the imposing Priory, standing all by itself, with a big graveyard – no. Other sorts of people went to the Priory, whom we did not know.

But to be just to Miss Whitworth, she was in reality the daughter of a clergyman and came from Wellingborough. She was of the family of Whitworth's flour and before she started a school she came to Dunstable as Governess to the younger children of Canon & Mrs. Baker, Canon Baker being the incumbent of the Priory.

There were only ten, at the most twelve, of us at Miss Whitworth's, sitting at three tables in the ground floor room that stretched the length of the house. First and foremost we learnt to read and write and to do sums. (Not arithmetic and certainly not maths – sums was the word). There was a proper set curriculum, following a laid-down practice. We learnt how to write clearly, how to put sentences together, how to spell, what was punctuation and grammar. To learn our tables, how to add and subtract, to multiply and to divide, what fractions were. The home truths of teaching. How to take dictation, to learn poetry, to recite.

In addition there was a large book from which the stories of history were read and told to us – Hereward the Wake, King Arthur were two. Children's stories were introduced – Grimm's Fairy Tales, The Pied Piper, Robin Hood, Peter Pan. England, Great Britain and the Romans were talked about and other people in other lands, like Eskimos and strange tribes in Africa. Bible stories were read and each morning started with a prayer and a hymn, Miss Whitworth playing on her piano. She was fond of music and was an ARCM. Drawing and handwork were part of our lessons, to be able to express ourselves, to follow simple rules. On a more active note, we had 'drill', with dumbells.

There was a great emphasis placed on Natural History. We were encouraged to know the flowers, to recognise birds and animals and talk about where we had been. I still have a book given to me – 'Butterflies' in the 'Shown to the Children' series – in which is inscribed, in Miss Whitworth's clear and precise hand-writing, my name and the notation 'Wild Flower Collection, Summer 1933'. Miss Whitworth actually was an authority on wild flowers and a valued member of The British Wild Flower Society, keeping the register of wild flowers for that association.

The garden at the back of the house was a long, narrow one and on dry days in the summer we were allowed out there, provided we behaved ourselves. There were skipping ropes supplied and we could generally run and jump about. Sometimes, on an afternoon, we went into the nearby recreation ground and attempted to play rounders, taken by Miss Whitworth's assistant, the pleasant Miss Harding, who was there for my first two years, and then the long-suffering Miss Pratt. There was an outing once a year to the Barton Hills and a picnic was taken.

Mention of Miss Pratt reminds me that she was completely opposite to her superior. She didn't look like a school-mistress in the slightest; she was comfortably built and she was inclined to let us giggle and laugh sometimes when she was reading a story from the history book. It brought her a gentle but firm admonition on one occasion – "Miss Pratt, could we have a little less noise, please, if you don't mind". But Miss Pratt had one big cross to bear, in connection with me.

My mother sometimes had old-fashioned ideas as to how her son should be clothed. She was also aware, rightly so, that Dunstable in winter was a cold place and that everyone should be properly wrapped up. I also suffered from chapped knees (not funny at all, only short trousers were worn then, no long ones for children of that age and chapped knees hurt). So at this particular time, in the middle months of winter, I had 'gaiters' to put on, which had a considerable number of buttons to do up (no zips, not yet heard of) and which took a considerable time so to do. Help was therefore needed. It was Miss Pratt's task to make sure that at the end of school each morning, to go home to dinner and again in the afternoon, all the children were properly clothed and looked after. The bane of Miss Pratt's life was my gaiters. She got so exasperated at the time taken on one occasion that she did suggest that perhaps my mother could clothe me in something else, though it was not put quite like that. I didn't like the wretched things, either, so it was a mutual feeling, but support for my mother led me not to express so outside our home. However, like the grey felt boy's hat I was forced to wear once, those gaiters did have a relatively short life, unlike my chaps.

Apart from two friends that came with me to the big school, I can only remember two other children at Miss Whitworth's over the three years that I was there. One was a fair-faced little girl in pigtails called Annabel (Annabel? Christabel? Not sure, some kind of 'bel' anyway) whom one day I decided I was going to marry. I told my mother this over dinner. "Are you, dear", she said, "that would be nice; will you have some more pudding?" So much for my important announcement. The other child was the 'Head girl', who shall remain nameless. Suffice to say that she was part of a well-known Dunstable family, who did a great deal for the town, and that she herself has given excellent and considerable service to the field of education.

Miss Whitworth was another Dunstable character, in her own way; once seen, never forgotten. No-one who went through that little school will forget her testimony of life. She did a good job for God.

Chapter 7 (2)

SCHOOL DAYS
THE GRAMMAR SCHOOL

From the September day in 1888 that Dunstable Grammar School opened its doors, under the headmastership of L. C. R. Thring, it became an integral part of Dunstable. It was an asset to the town and the town accepted it as such. The building was in the town, it was of the town and it brought credit to the town. The masters played their part in the civic and social affairs of the town and all its events were reported in great detail in the local Dunstable paper. A big event like Speech Day, which incorporated the Founders' Day service and Sports Day on the school playing field would take up two whole pages. Dunstable was proud of its Grammar School and rightly so.

It was not one of the leading schools of the country. It was not expected to be and it never set out to be in the same category as a major public school, even though the school song, referring to Eton and Harrow, says 'Wait awhile, we may yet have a bard of our own'. It was not one of the topmost grammar schools, although it had been classified early on as a minor public school and boys came from distant parts of the world to be boarded there. But it *was* a grammar school, a good grammar school and it gave a sound all-round education aligned with sporting activities of note. It taught courtesy, politeness and the basic truths of life. And because of the masters over the years and a lot of the boys who went there it was a character school, with a happy atmosphere.

I was fortunate again to be there when it still had that atmosphere and when the masters were characters in themselves, even though, as I understand it, the first thirty years of the twentieth century were outstanding. Certainly I am thankful that my parents, by dint of saving and foregoing things themselves, managed to send me there. I am proud to be an Old Dunstablian, I don't mind saying so, and I only wish, along with thousands of other Old Boys, that there was still a Dunstable Grammar School.

An aerial view of Dunstable Grammar School, about 1952, but virtually unchanged. Immediately behind the school in the photograph is the swimming bath where it looks as though, by the crowd there, a special event is taking place. Over to the right are the gymnasium and the wood-work room, behind which lies Dog Kennel Path, continuing on past the southern extremity of Waterlow's factory, top left. In the school grounds, this side of the clump of trees, can be seen the rifle shooting butts, moved from their pre-war central position. To the left of the swimming bath is 'The New' building, additional classrooms opened in 1924 but always referred to by that title. The little path at the back of this building winds across to Ashton Lodge, out of the picture. In the High Street itself, to the left of the school, stand two shops. The right hand one is closed up, but the other, with the blind down, was that of 'Daddy' Barnes.

The Speech Hall, with some of the Hankey Gold Medal plaques around the walls.   *[DGS(1)*

Joining the Prep. School in the Autumn of 1933 was a happy start, which was just as well, because at the end of the summer holidays here was a big school and an utterly different environment for me. I was, however, more than ready for it and I seemed to fit in without any problem. The Prep. School, although it had its two form rooms and its joint meeting room in the creeper-covered Ashton Lodge, with its own grass lawn and flower beds outside, was part of the main school and every morning we met with the rest of the school in the Speech Hall (with the names of all the boys that had won the Hankey Gold Medal each year from 1890, inscribed in gold lettering on a brown background in panels on the walls, high up, looking down on us) for morning assembly and prayers. The forty to forty-five boys that made up the Prep. School would then repair to Ashton Lodge for lessons. But the entrance and exit gates of the school were the same for the Prep. as everyone else, so was the playing field and so were the school hours. The hours, of course, embraced the full six days of the week, with lessons in the morning only on Wednesdays and Saturdays. The half-days then were for school matches. In the summer and in the lighter days of term there were two lessons in the afternoon, followed by games, but in the winter, when it was dark, games were played first and the two lessons were taken from half-past three to five o'clock. Prep.

existed every night of the week and over the week-end, a great deal of it.

Dress of the day was a uniform grey shirt, with grey shorts, long grey socks and black shoes. The tie was a short woollen one of horizontal stripes and the coat was a dark blue blazer with the school initials on the pocket. After two years, when I had left the Prep. and was in the senior school, it was an Eton collar in the Shells and the Third form, up to the age of fourteen, and a proper matching coat and trousers. Caps had to be worn during term at all times outside the school, although in the summer term some of the boys wore boaters. I had one in the early days, but I was not all that enthusiastic about it – it got knocked off very quickly, for one reason. Ties were either school ties of chocolate and blue, the school's colours, or house ties of various hues. My house tie for instance was yellow and black stripes.

Every boy was expected to behave himself outside the school, in the town, on public transport (a considerable number of boys came to school on a bus or on the train from Luton) and elsewhere. There was to be no unseemly behaviour and this included eating from anything or drinking a bottle of pop. The right dress and behaviour was strictly upheld and the prefects saw to that as well as any master. I thought I was perfectly safe, one late Saturday afternoon standing at the bottom of Beech Hill in Luton waiting for a bus, when I was in the Fourth, eating two pennyworth of chips. Not so. Called up to the Prefects' Study on the Monday morning, at break-time, there followed 100 lines on the avoidance of devouring chips on the public highway – "in your best handwriting, please". Dropping litter was almost as punishable an offence as being late for school or not doing your prep. Actually we never really thought of dropping anything on the pavement or elsewhere – it just wasn't done. Would I could dish out 100 lines now to all the schoolchildren (and others) who drop paper bags, cartons, cans, without a second thought on the pavement and in the road where I live now!

The master in charge of the Prep. was Mr. C. L. Harris, a man totally dedicated to the school and to the boys for whom he was responsible. He also served as a housemaster of Thompson House, one of the four houses of the main school that were named after famous masters of earlier years (Apthorp, Brown, Thompson and Thring). C. L. Harris was particularly good with boys of fourteen and under and once again I was fortunate in having him as my first form master and then as the master that looked after Under-14 cricket. I was also in Thompson, so our paths crossed almost every day, for one reason or another.

I owe him a lot, not the least of which was the introduction and insight he gave me to English literature, to poetry and to the English language. Here were, suddenly, books that I had never heard of, adventure stories waiting to be read, the lilt of rhythm and rhyme of epic ballads in verse.

The Prep School, Summer Term, 1935. Forms 1 and 2 outside Ashton Lodge. Waterlow's chimney on the right.
From memory, left to right:
Back row: Kingham, Higgins ii, Wallis, Harmer, Weatherill, Ostler, Higgins i, Grover, Colvin (?), Wilks, Clegg
Third row: Willis, Morris iii, Cooper, Warren, Bourne, Bond, Cleveley, French ii, Wilkinson, Cawcutt, Weston
Second row: Steerwood, Watson, Castle, Plowman, Barrett ii, Barrett i, Mr. C. L. Harris, Gauntlet, Webdale, Thody, Briars, Cartwright
Front row: Puckey, Brookes, Morris iv, Headey, Croot (?), Woods, Harrison, Blundell, Fellingham, Dinsdale.

No wonder that form prizes in the Prep. School centred round books like 'The Jungle Book' and 'Huckleberry Finn' and 'Wonder Tales from Many Lands'.

We also learnt, very quickly, team spirit; being part of a team, supporting that team. No individual, however big a part he played in the team, was bigger than the team itself. The boy who was not particularly good, but tried hard, was as important as the star of the team. Everyone could play their part for the benefit of the team. It would have done to-day's Prima Donnas of our sporting world a lot of good if they had been in the Prep. School of Dunstable Grammar.

One of Mr. Harris's strictures was that in the summer term the Prep. would produce a play or an historical pageant on the lawn outside Ashton Lodge. Every boy would take part (the team spirit again), it was an educational part of the Prep's activities and it would have to be good, because it would be attended by proud mums and dads (well, mostly mums – it was an afternoon performance, only done once) together with younger brothers and sisters. But enjoyable also. And so it was really in the end, though Mr. Harris, whose brother was Christopher Fry, the playwright, shook his head in despair on many occasions in the weeks and days that led up to THE DAY. Came the time on a warm summer's afternoon, with the audience sitting down one side on hard chairs, and frantic adjustments by the hard-working wardrobe mistress to some of the young actors' apparel, it all came right.

I remember two scenes in particular in which I was involved. The first occasion was when I was Captain Hook. I thought this was a wonderful part. Here I was in a pirate's outfit, with a black eye-patch and a red 'kerchief on my head, wielding a thin, silver painted wooden cutlass and stamping up and down, shouting away and making all sorts of terrible noises, as people were made to walk the plank. The only thing was that I got rather near the audience, in the front of which, sitting on the grass, were some of these little brothers and sisters. Such was the power of the cutlass waving and the snarls and fearsome looks that were going on, that I'm afraid I made one little boy cry, he was so frightened. Well, there you are, there's nothing like playing a part successfully.

The second occasion was when I really *did* look the part, quite accidentally. This time we were enacting an English Pageant-through-the-Ages type of production. The opening scene was one of Roman Britain. A young Briton would walk on looking about him as though he feared something. He would be pounced on by three Roman soldiers, a fight would ensue and he would then be dragged, struggling, to the Centurion, who would make a speech and mete out some unjust punishment. I was to be the young Briton.

Two days before the pageant was to take place I was allowed, by special dispensation for a Prep. School boy, to have my first cricket net, with the Shell forms. It was entirely my own fault that I was standing inside the net, where I should not have been, when I got hit by a cricket ball over the eye. There were a lot of stars shooting around suddenly and momentarily it knocked me out. I came to at the back of the net with Mr. H. J. Butters, that very fine master beloved by so many generations of boys (sometimes after they had left school when they had got over the feeling of 'Benjamin descending from on high' and fully realised his worth), standing over me. "Are you alright, lad?" he asked with concern. I nodded. "Oh, good" he said "have a cherry", where-upon he offered me an open bag of cherries that he had brought to the nets.

The result of this blow, of course, was a real shiner. I will leave aside the reaction of my mother when I got home and sheepishly walked into the kitchen, and jump two days to the pageant. By this time the colouring was at its best. It really was a very good black eye and it was realised, for those not in the know (i.e. the audience) that it could well be the result of a fight. So the scene was changed very slightly, there was a noise of a fight off-stage and I was dragged in, still fighting, until I fell to the ground in an appropriate place before the watching company. I was then hauled to my feet facing the audience before being marched to the Centurion. The result was quite good, really. Gasps went up, ladies' hands went to their mouths and the effect made me even prouder of my black eye than I was already (after all, it was my first one). I like to think that pageant got off to a realistic start . . . with the Wars of the Roses still to come, too.

I am not an actor, I never have been one and I had no burning desire to be one, but I did join the Dramatic Society after leaving the Prep. (Puck in Midsummer Night's Dream was my pièce de résistance) and on one notable occasion I was a girl pierrot, with three other 'girls', in an infamous Glee Club production in which other Dunstable folk joined. There was a strong bond between school and town and this concert, as part of the Golden Jubilee celebrations, was only one of many events, both at the school and in the town, where representatives of the two came together, over the years.

Certainly the town knew when anything special was on, aside from the normal coming and going of boys in term time to and from the school and up to the playing field and back, emphasised even more in High Street North (a bit like Waterlow's really, – there were set times when action took place and the streets were extra busy).

Speech Day was one of these special events when we were supposed to be on our best behaviour and to ensure that our clothes were especially clean (to some that was quite impossible). The whole school walked in a crocodile fashion up the High Street, down Church Street and into the Priory. The Rector took the service, the sermon was

The cast of 'A Midsummer Night's Dream'. Puck seems to have one ear flap up and one ear flap down. It was written of his performance that he 'seemed to enjoy thoroughly his elfin pranks'. No further comment. [DGS(2)

The Pierrot Troupe. Mr.Coales, left at the back and Mr. Boskett, far right are the two masters present. In the centre, seated, is Florrie Perry, who played a great part in musical circles in and around Dunstable, both in pre and post-war years, and guided and helped a whole host of young people. She often assisted at school concerts, taking the soprano lead, particularly for the Glee Club performances in the Easter term. [DGS(2)

A performance by the Glee Club, in the Speech Hall. The stars in the front row, from left to right:– Mr. C. L. Harris, Miss Florrie Perry, Miss Doreen Lester, Mr. Cyril Tibbett, Mr. W. D. Coales and a gentleman who escapes all recognition. Old Boys of pre-war vintage will spot Messrs. Lack, Cadle and Le Huray in the back row.
[DGS(1)

generally preached by a visiting clergyman, the headmaster and the head boy read lessons and the final hymn was always 'Jerusalem'. In the afternoon, prize-giving, preceded by the headmaster's report for the year, was generally held in the old Town Hall, though I also remember it in our own Speech Hall. On the platform were all the masters, wearing their gowns, the Governors (which included little white-haired Mr. Wallace, of carnation fame) and the visiting speaker. His obligatory request to the Head for a half-holiday raised the biggest cheer of the afternoon, but not necessarily the loudest noise. This was reserved, at the end, for the singing of the school song, a ballad-type composition written three years before the turn of the century and with a rousing tune and chorus, made all the more rousing by Mr. Leslie Boskett's rendering of it on the piano. It was a haunting school song, once sung, never forgotten. I used to put my heart and soul into the singing of this and I was not alone, not by the proverbial long chalk.

If the sound of that song was heard well outside the Town Hall, in the High Street and through the cross roads, then the noise of boys cheering on the School 1st XV at a rugger match on the playing field, tucked away between West Parade and West Street, also reverberated around in no uncertain manner.

[DGS(1)]

Speech Day in the old Town Hall, the headmaster – Mr. A. F. R. Evans – presiding. A 1937 scene.

The philosophy of Dunstable Grammar School about sport was quite simple. Unless you were excused it on genuine medical grounds, you played it. And if you were not playing in the match yourself on a Wednesday or a Saturday afternoon, and there was a 1st XV rugby or a 1st XI hockey or cricket match at home, then in the senior school you supported that team and were expected to be present. Not expected, you had to be and house prefects would take a roll-call of the members of their house on the field to make sure you were there (and it was not just 100 lines if you were missing).

The school had a very fine reputation for the quality of its hockey, nurtured by H. J. Butters, who had played for his native Staffordshire and who turned out for School v Club matches at right back – heaven help any left-winger who tried to get the better of H.J.B., if the ball wasn't taken then that forward had shins much more sore than when he started the game. However, rugby lent itself to a more passionate reception than hockey, so when the rest of the school were watching the 1st XV a lot of passion was aroused off the field of play as well as on it. There were several times during the course of a game when those on the touchline let out a great, baying 'Scho-o-o-o-l' at the top of their voices, letting it go on for several minutes. When the 1st XV pack was encamped near their opponents' goal line, the word 'heel' got the same treatment. This sound swelled out of the ground to West Street on one side and down West Parade on the other, over the back streets of Princes, Victoria and Edward and down to High Street North itself. So in Dunstable there was no doubt what was going on when that noise was heard.

There were two special event days in which townsfolk participated by coming to watch. Although the playing field was private property the big wooden gates in West Street, where cars could be driven in, and the little iron gate in West Parade, which was the common entrance for all members of the school, were always open when matches and events were on and visitors were always welcome.

One of these events was Sports Day, which was the athletic meeting of the year – all the races from the 100 yard dash for the Prep. School right through the various ages and distances to the Senior mile, plus the high jump and the long jump. There was no room for the javelin or throwing the discus or other such events. All during the week heats were run, so that Sports Day really consisted of the finals, unless wet weather caused a few semi-finals to be run also. It was a busy scene, taking place on a Saturday afternoon early in the summer term and the field was full of participants, time-keepers, parents and visitors with order always coming out of what could have been chaos. This was where a few of the masters who were not really all that interested in sport took an invaluable part – time-keeping, marshalling and generally organising. It meant that those masters who were in charge of XIs and XVs throughout the school could be in the background and enjoy the scene, taking the opportunity too, to talk to parents and their friends. I took part in Sports Day, but to little effect. However, a boy was also running for his house, not just for individual glory, so points could be notched up here and there which could make all the difference to winning the House Cup or not.

The other big event was the Old Boys' Cricket Match on the last Saturday of the summer term and therefore right at the end of the school year. This, to me, was a big day, long before I had the privilege of playing in it and not just because of the fact that the long summer holidays lay ahead, although that meant, in turn, no more maths, no more chemistry, no more physics (my apologies to all those responsible for those subjects) and the yearly exams over. True, there was THE REPORT still to come and be opened, but with a bit of luck there would be some plus marks to outweigh the minuses that undoubtedly would be there.

After morning school on that Saturday of the Old Boys' Match, nearly every boy in the school took a chair from the Speech Hall up to the ground and encircled the field with them. Apart from a couple of benches and the seats within the pavilion enclosure itself, which were obviously reserved, there was no seating on the ground and with the whole school there (at least until the tea interval), Old Boys, parents, masters and wives, well-wishers, it was very necessary.

It was a happy scene, enhanced by the nature of the match itself. I would hold the big boys of the 1st XI, from the Sixth Form and the Upper Fifth, in awe and watch their progress keenly; cheer when an Old Boy's wicket fell but applaud also when a boundary was hit by those returning. Such was the balance of the game of cricket for me, even at an early age. In some way the game itself had got through to me, what it was really all about. I remember one particular stroke from an Old Boy (one who had made his mark in minor counties cricket for Buckinghamshire) one year that brought every spectator on the ground to his or her feet. It was a straight six hit clean through the top window of a house in West Parade and it left a round hole just the size of a cricket ball. There was no other shattering of glass at all. The ground itself, as a cricket ground, was a good-sized one and that ball had to cover a good distance. There was, of course, an immediate rush of small boys to the boundary hedge to view the damage and the poor umpire, as the boys were right behind the wicket, was kept busy for a moment clearing them away.

There was another instance that stays in the memory, this in the 1938 special Golden Jubilee match against the M.C.C. – the school fast bowler, who was already playing for Bedfordshire, bowling the captain of Northants first ball. "Poetry in motion, poetry in motion", his

'Under 14' rugger – perhaps the socks didn't need to be pulled up with that length of the shorts.

bowling was described to me by one of his team-mates in much later years. I am also told that when the same fast bowler removed the Reverend gentleman who was captain of the M.C.C. that day – and who was good enough to have opened for England some ten years earlier – the last ball before tea, the Reverend gentleman uttered a four-letter word, heard clearly as far as cover-point, that was not generally heard on the playing field of Dunstable Grammar School in those days . . . or any school playing field, come to that!

The School field – The Mill Field of old – was an enchanting place for me, in summer. I loved being up there at any time, in all terms, watching in the younger days, then mostly playing, particularly when I got into the 'Under 14' games and then matches. Suddenly, there was another wide-ranging aspect in life and I used to crowd into the passage way between the Speech Hall and the Quad, where the notice boards were, to see if I had been selected for the next match. The day was made if I had, even with a double maths period to come or the unequal struggle with Latin verbs an immediate prospect.

I knew very little outside Dunstable, really. We had no car, and holidays away at the sea were very few and far between. It was walking or catching a bus to walk and picnic somewhere. The only place I came to know well was by making friends, through our church, with a boy who came from Bury St. Edmunds and quite often after the initial 'allowed to go away by myself', I would spend some days with him in that East Anglian town. So to suddenly be a member of a team, to

112

represent the school and be taken to matches in one of Mr. Costin's coaches, was a great experience. Thus we went to play at Luton Modern, The Cedars, St. George's Harpenden, Hitchin G.S., Bedford Modern, Caldicott, Wellbury Park and later at Aldenham, Berkhamsted, Royal Masonic Bushey, RCTS Pinner, Christ's College Finchley. . . .

But naturally, it is the home field that one remembers. I must have played there hundreds and hundreds of times; I must have walked up there well over a thousand times. I was exceedingly lucky that I lived so close to the school itself. I literally just had to walk out of the shop in the morning, cross over the road and some fifty yards further on I was there. (However, I can remember three other boys who lived even closer). So to the playing field was only a five-minute walk. Along from the shop, up Union Street, along Victoria Street, past one side of Mr. Robinson's nurseries, up the alley and into West Parade. Or a variation thereof. When I was not playing myself there was often a call at a little sweet shop on the corner of Princes Street and West Parade. This was owned by a Mrs. Dixon (sister-in-law to our Mr. Dixon, next door) and the shop had been converted from the front room of the house. Mrs. Dixon was a white-haired lady with a high-pitched voice who always wore a pinafore and was another person who always appeared from the back, when the shop door clanged. Her husband, 'Speedy' Dixon, used to walk round Dunstable at a very slow pace selling flowers that he had bought at Robinson's nurseries.

The Mill Field was an open field, but it also enjoyed seclusion, bounded as it was by the large terraced houses of West Parade and the brick wall of the back gardens of the houses in West Street at either end; the mill itself in one corner; two corner, small spinneys of trees; hedges and gardens and a line of trees, in the middle of which was the long jump run, by the side of the pavilion. Behind that pavilion ran the path known as Leighton Gap, a short cut between West Street and West Parade, where it came out alongside Miss Gurney's dress shop. Leighton Gap was also bordered by a black corrugated fence, behind which lay Mr. Seamons' extensive nurseries, with their greenhouses. Dunstable had a lot of nurseries for a small town, as besides those belonging to Mr. Robinson and Mr. Seamons there were five others in the Downs Road/Blows Road/ Borough Road area, one in Church Street, two in Chiltern Road and Mr. Larking in Victoria Street, at the top of Clifton Road, which we also used to go to. Of all those only one in Chiltern Road remains.

So with the open but enclosed nature of the ground it was almost free from the cold winds and the fresh breezes that I seem to have experienced since, standing on school playing fields, particularly Berkhamsted. The ground looked its best in summer, with all the changing

I was not in the Cadet Corps, but I include this photograph of the Corps being inspected one winter's day because it was taken on the school playing field and it shows the pavilion, alas no more. The master-in-charge of the Cadet Corps, Mr. A. C. Wadsworth, can be seen, third from the left in the forefront, talking to visiting brass. [DGS(1)

. . . but this one must not be missed. The never-to-be forgotten Regimental Sergeant-Major Odell with his smallest cadet, November 1932. [DGS(1)

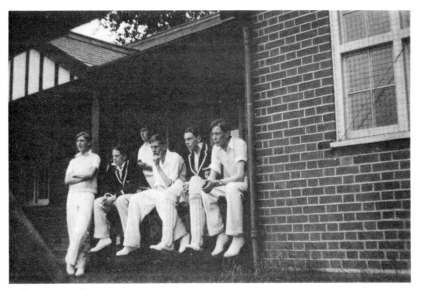

A summer afternoon
From left to right: Peter Nye, Colin Swain, Sam Rogers (in background) Derek
Brown, myself, John Briars. Two of these six were killed whilst serving in H.M.
Forces.

shades of green and also because there was an uninterrupted view, with no rugby posts or hockey goals, anywhere.

The pavilion was not a big one, but like the school itself it had character and it blended in with the ground. It was, in fact, a very simple one, not designed to be grandiose by having a balcony and upstairs facilities and changing rooms all over the place and tables where thirty or so people could sit down to eat. It had width rather than depth and a sloping tiled roof with windows all along the front. It had one large middle room, with a wooden floor, which looked out on to the ground and where tea could be served in a buffet fashion in the summer. On one side was the changing room (where very little changing took place, boys and visiting sides walked up from the school in their playing kit and walked back down again, mud and all) which disappeared into obscure toilets and on the other a little room where tea could be prepared and where the tea urns were stored. Outside the main room was a small covered-in sitting area and then an enclosure of grass before the wooden pavilion railings. It was all very delightful sitting or standing in and around that pavilion and I never lost the thrill of going down the wide concrete path in the middle to play for the school at rugger, or with a hockey stick in my hand, wearing the chocolate and blue shirt, or walking out to bat. I don't think any of the Old Boys did, otherwise they

115

would not have come back, from near and far, to play in the special matches of each term.

The pavilion had two other attributes. Around the walls of the main room were ranged the photographs of all the school cricket 1st XIs going back some considerable way. Some were faded, some of the names difficult to read, but we looked at those photos over and over again. They had some kind of magnetic appeal. So we would find the lad who had had six seasons in the 1st XI, we would find fathers who now had sons there, we would find uncles and in my case a brother-in-law, we would find names and faces that were not of English extraction, we would find the well-known names. We searched in vain for Gary Cooper (obviously not a cricketer). We wondered whether our photographs would be there, in years to come. Little did we know. . . .

The other attribute was more mundane. In the little tea room there was a hatch that in the summer, on school match days, was opened so that the watching boys could avail themselves of something to drink. Not tea, of course, but bottles of pop. So there were a few crates of Tizer and drinks like fizzy lemonade and American Cream Soda. After all, watching and playing around a bit in the nearby spinney and behind the high jump pit was thirsty work. It was well patronised by the younger boys and to have a few pennies in the pocket to share a bottle with two or three friends, for each of us to have a swig now and again, wiping the top with our hands when we had done so, was part of the enjoyment of the afternoon.

(I should think by now that the impression will have been given that, what with 'Daddy' Barnes' shop, Mrs. Dixon's shop and this last one in the pavilion we ate a considerable number of sweets and drank a lot of pop. Probably quite right. It was possible, actually, for a boy to buy something during mid-morning break at the official school tuck-shop near the Masters' Common Room, presided over by the inimitable Sergeant-Major Odell, make his second purchase of the day as he left the school gates with Mr. Barnes, pick up the odd item from Mrs. Dixon and finish off by the pavilion. Some did just that).

Very occasionally, now, if I happen to go along West Parade or along Leighton Gap, I stop and look across that same field, because it is still there, although there are differences. Over by the mill, there are now houses backing on to the field and along that side there are changes. There is no longer any entrance in West Street, more buildings stand on that stretch. The little wooden score box, over the other side opposite the pavilion and which had many initials carved into the thick wooden flap where the scorers placed their books, has gone – quite understandably, as it was somewhat decrepit. The big shed by the pavilion, which housed the mowers and all the sporting equipment and the pavilion itself have gone, that favourite pavilion, which is inexcusable – let go by the educational authorities so that in the end it had to be pulled down. It should have been a listed building, that pavilion, not one to be disregarded and let fall into disrepair.

The field looks forlorn, the boys have gone. And yet, for me, a hundred ghosts flit to and fro. I can see the scenes of yesteryear, I can hear the voices of days gone by. Where are they all, now, those friends? The Second World War scattered them and some did not return, one of whom I particularly remember and who lived but a hundred yards away from where I stand. And those who did come back? One is in Australia, one in Canada, one in the United States. They are in Devon, in Cornwall, in East Anglia, in Yorkshire, in Worcestershire, in Derbyshire, in Sussex, in Kent, in Cheshire and Lancashire, in Dorset, in the length and breadth of the land. Some of them are known, others I know not where. Not for me, I am afraid, not for any of us, really, will I be able to say . . .

> 'I will hold my house in the high wood
> Within a walk of the sea,
> And the men that were boys when I was a boy
> Shall sit and drink with me.'
> . . . .

No chapter on the Grammar School that I remember can be written without talking about the masters, because nearly all of them had some influence on me and the time I spent at this school was after all a large and important chunk of my early life in Dunstable. All of them, knowingly or perhaps unknowingly, set the pattern that whatever is taken out of life, in any walk, something must be put back. Theirs was a philosophy that with the greatest respect, all teachers of the young would do well to follow today, in these apparently turbulent times of education.

Some masters I knew better and came into contact with more than others, simply because they were my form master, or house master, or the master in charge of a particular XI or XV. I have already spoken of Mr. Harris and referred to Mr. Butters, both of whom played an important part in my education. But no mention of H. J. Butters can really do justice to the man. He taught geography, which I enjoyed, he was the P.T. master and he was the master in charge of games. His house was at the West Parade corner of the playing field by the little gate. He was a strict disciplinarian and no boy, if he had the slightest grain of common sense in him, ever tried to get the better of H.J.B. You could get away with things, sometimes, with two or three other masters, but not Mr. Butters.

He was the first to encourage a boy who had no outstanding talents. And he had a kind and understanding heart, particularly if he knew you were doing your best. He understood, for example, that a young boy

The Common Room, 1938
From left to right: **back row:** *F. R. Speke, F. M. Bancroft, R. L. Poirier, A. C. Wadsworth, W. N. Brock, F. Cadle*
Seated: *C. L. Harris, L. A. Boskett, W. D. Coales, A. F. R. Evans (Headmaster), H. J. Butters, C. P. Le Huray,*
W. T. Lack.
[DGS(2)

batting in the cricket nets, facing a hard straight ball coming down fast, had a general tendency to back away to leg. He had a simple remedy. A bucket of water was placed immediately behind the legs. That cured the habit fast, and no-one lost face. Coming from Staffordshire, Mr. Butters naturally tended to support Stoke City F.C. From an early term, he knew my affinity to Arsenal. I think he was slightly amused at my depth of feeling, but I think also that he thought, well, here's a boy who has a great love and support for his team and is not likely to be swayed and therefore should not be looked at lightly. Anyway, he said one day that if ever Stoke City had their away fixture against Arsenal in the holidays, he would take me to see the match. Three years later they did and I reminded him politely of the conversation. There was no deliberation whatever; there was an instant reply. "Right", he said "off we go". So we did. He took me up on the train from Luton, we watched the game at Highbury, standing on the terraces on a bitterly cold December day and he then treated me to a hot meal at a restaurant somewhere off Piccadilly Circus before returning home. Arsenal won 4–0, yes, but I didn't remember that day for the result alone. . . .

The third of the masters with whom I had a lot to do was Mr. Bancroft – F.M.B. A Welshman of true Welsh fervour, but not overdoing it, he was the senior history master, taught divinity and, as I came through the school, the master in charge of rugby and cricket. I enjoyed history and, being brought up to go to church, divinity did not bore me. Mr. Bancroft was a big man in every way and another strict disciplinarian but, again, kind and understanding. He was also the sort of man that you could sit on the ground with, as I did, in the break in a rugger game on a late, warm September day and just have a chat. We were on the same wavelength. Although he came to the school much later than Mr. Butters, Old Boys would often speak about Bancroft and Butters in the same breath.

I can recall many moments with Mr. Bancroft, including facing his two types of bowling – his innocent, beguiling slow spinners, tossed high in the air and his 'faster' stuff coming in from the West Street end with every fibre of his ample frame quivering. But there was one happening that I particularly remember, quite understandably, as will be appreciated.

If there were no matches on a Wednesday afternoon in the summer term then the 1st XI and the 2nd XI would join forces to play a full game between themselves. It was properly scored and was invaluable practice out in the middle as distinct from having nets (which we had twice a week, in any case). It so happened, on that particular afternoon, that, batting first I scored runs and was not out, with another batsman also, when we came in. Any boy, playing cricket, wants to know how many runs he has scored if he has had a reasonable innings. We never knew our individual total, as there was nowhere to put it up, so I asked the scorer when he wandered over from the little box. "97" was the reply, which Mr. Bancroft happened, by chance, to overhear. There was an instant decision, although no action was really necessary at all. "Come on, everybody", F.M.B. called out, "out again, quick, as we were". He made everyone come out on to the field of play again, before the other side's innings began, so that I had the chance of getting the other three runs, which, thank goodness, I did. It was not all that important, really, it was not a match against another school that would be recorded in history, but Mr. Bancroft knew what it would mean to a schoolboy and gave him that opportunity.

Then there was W. D. Coales ('Codey') second master and occupier of the chemistry laboratories. Mr. Coales *was* chemistry and chemistry was Mr. Coales. Many are the tales told about his chemistry experiments. A feature at the school, seemingly since it first began, he was an active man, very quick on his toes. He took part in the aforementioned Glee Club concert and brought the house down with his spirited rendering of 'I made 'em do the cake walk'. No record of the Grammar School would ever be complete without him, his contribution was considerable.

Where Mr. Coales invented chemistry, so to speak, Wilfred Lack lived in the physics laboratory, close by. He had a little room in the corner of that lab. and no-one quite knew what was in it. From time to time he would disappear there. Rumour and counter rumour abounded, but the puzzle was never satisfactorily solved. Mr. Lack was also in charge of the swimming pool and of swimming. He was a man of many parts, doing a great number of things around the school, including teaching woodwork. He is forever immortalised for his nickname ('Fudger') and for his drawing of a dotted line on the blackboard. He would draw an ordinary line, wet his finger and then make breaks in the chalk. Mr. Lack, later on, gave great service to the town, becoming the Mayor of Dunstable, an Alderman and the holder of an O.B.E. He was always willing to help in special events, both at the school and in the town. The old Dunstable Borough Council, in due course, gave him the honour of Alderman Emeritus.

Leslie Boskett (the same Mr. Boskett of 'The Square') was the senior maths master as well as a brilliant pianist and a fearless hockey umpire. His opening phrase at any lesson, in his own dialect, was "Now, now, boys" and he had the extraordinary habit, when taking a new piece of chalk from the cupboard, of breaking off the top and tossing it with unerring accuracy out of one of the top windows of the tall classroom. He was thus known as 'Toss' and there were times when we used to hide the used chalk in order to see this performance carried out. He, too, took part in much activity in Dunstable, participating in concerts all

The Science Block, built in 1907. /DGS(1)

The Chemistry Laboratory, the domain of the mercurial Mr. Coales. /DGS(1)

121

over the place as well as being the organist every Sunday for the church. He was a great organiser. I am grateful to him, amongst other things, for getting me through School Certificate Algebra, which he ought to have ranked as one of his outstanding achievements.

Freddie Cadle was a quiet man and I suspect under-rated in his value to the school. A bachelor who lived at Ashton Lodge in term time, he was the second master in Thompson House, his main subject Latin, although he took English as well. He always carried into any class a knobbly, short stick, and a cardboard, open file of papers which bulged outwards and always seemed likely to fall out all over the place. He used to walk around making music in his head and he was a writer of fairy stories. When I was confined to my bedroom at home for a month with scarlet fever, Mr. Cadle wrote out the whole instructions for me as to how to play Patience, which was no mean feat, in order to help me pass the time. On the more active side Mr. Cadle played and looked after Fives and I had much pleasure, on a Friday afternoon, playing this fascinating and exhausting game in one of the two Rugby Fives courts in the quad, at the side of the swimming pool.

Like Mr. Cadle, Fred Speke hailed from Gloucestershire and was another quiet man, but totally dedicated and very much liked. Coming three years after I had started, our paths never crossed all that much as house and form and year of teaching did not meet, but when I did talk with him I found again we were on the same wavelength. Many years later an Old Boy, whom I didn't know really, said to me that one of his outstanding memories of the school was Mr. Speke and the help he gave this boy in his attempt to swim. The boy found it difficult, but persevered and when at long last he managed a length of the baths, "Do you know", said the Old Boy, "Mr. Speke was so pleased he gave me a shilling".

Mr. A. C. Wadsworth, of the precise English voice, was the epitome of an English gentleman. He taught English, too, amongst other subjects, but he is probably best remembered as the producer of some excellent school plays and for being the head of the school Cadet Corps. Although not specifically under the control of Mr. Wadsworth, but with his support and liaison, the Corps, with invaluable assistance from Old Boys, had a very fine drum and bugle band, which paraded at church services throughout the year, on Speech Day and at special civic services and events, where they were much in demand, as well as participating in tournaments outside the county. They were a stirring sight and sound, marching through the town and at the end giving an 'eyes right' salute to the school as they reached it on the way back. Mr. Wadsworth also owned a little Austin Seven car, which he parked in the school quad and which was the object of schoolboy pranks on more than one occasion. Like Mr. Lack he was also to be honoured and received the M.B.E.

Miss M. Draper   [DGS(2)

Little Mr. Le Huray, the Channel Islander who made his home in Dunstable, was the German master – ironic that he should teach the language of the nation that was to occupy his homeland; he had a shock of grey hair, a little, bristling moustache and walked with his feet at forty-five degrees. M. Poirier, the French master (there is often one master in a school that a boy does not get on with – M. Poirier and I did not see eye to eye). 'Badger' Brock from Wales who often questioned, with suitable action, the mental stability of the boy he was talking to and who was failing to comprehend; he lies in the peace and quiet of Totternhoe churchyard. Mr. Hedges, part-time 'Singing' master, taking lessons in the Lecture Room, with its ascending rows of benches and with the boys bellowing out sea shanties and songs from a Boosey & Hawkes cloth book, as well as hymns that we would be singing at morning assembly. The tall and elegant Miss Draper, a Victorian lady who dwelt amongst us twice a week for Art lessons.

All these masters were under the headship of Mr. A.F.R. Evans, who, although I saw him daily, at assembly and also at school home matches, I never knew well. To me he was a man aloof, but having said that I know he ran an efficient school and his staff were very loyal to him. I am sure he knew much more about me than I did of him.

On the last day of the school year, one summer, after our final assembly and with everybody departing I was crossing the almost deserted quad. Over by the memorial library there was a lad, who was in the Upper Fifth, quietly crying. He was a boy who had been somewhere in the middle of the class, not particularly good at games and who had left no outstanding mark on his school life. But he was well liked. Mr. Bancroft was trying to comfort him. "What's the matter, —?" he said. The boy dried his eyes, smiled a wan smile and replied . . . "I'm leaving today, sir. I don't want to leave. I've been so happy here".

The School from the Quad. The nearest five first-floor windows were the dormitories for the boarders. The large window on the right, at the edge of the photograph, part of the library. *[DGS(1)*

Part of the War Memorial Library, around 1930, given to the school by the Old Dunstablians' Club in memory of those pupils killed in the Great War. *[DGS(1)*

Chapter 8

THE ZOO

Whipsnade Zoo, when it opened in May 1931, made a great impact on Dunstable. News before then that there was going to be built, on the edge of the Downs and above the village of Whipsnade, a revolutionary type zoo, was a major talking point and brought considerable surprise. I don't think that it had quite the same impact as the amazement felt by the good people of St. Helena in 1815 when they learnt that the great Napoleon was to be exiled amongst them or the instantaneous reaction of delight that we felt that Coronation morning in early June 1953 when we opened our papers and read that Everest had been conquered.

But there was an impact, on the town itself, on the tradesmen, on families and, of course, on children. Suddenly, when it had opened and was proving an instant success, with thousands flocking to it, there was somewhere near Dunstable for a change ("Yes, you know, Whipsnade Zoo. It's near Dunstable"). For many years now, Dunstable had no real claim to modern fame. Dunstable was near Luton, or near St. Albans, or even near London. It was always 'near' something or some place. Now there was Whipsnade Zoo, near Dunstable.

Whipsnade, established by the London Zoological Society, was a zoo way ahead of its time, long before the Safari Parks came into being. In its five hundred acres the aim was to exhibit and maintain animals and birds as near as possible to their natural surroundings, rather than coop them up in cages or small dens, as in other zoos, thereby helping to preserve the species. Thus the wide, open paddocks where they could graze in comfort, the big attractive enclosures, the use of the tall-tree woods, the well constructed ponds; the whole embellished by thatched shelters and pleasant rides and the natural open hillside, where wallabies often roamed free.

For all those people who visited the Zoo in its early years, it was a wonderful experience and education to actually see those inmates from all over the world in the first place and secondly in such a natural

The entrance to Whipsnade Zoo, when it first opened. As you swing round to the right, a little further on, on the left, was the natural wood where the wolves were first situated, roaming around between the shadows of the tall trees. [WZ

habitat. Not least to the children and certainly not to me. In those early months there was always news of further animals arriving, and there was that memorable day when a whole lot of animals, from Bostock's menagerie, arrived in a train at the lower station (Dunstable North) en route for the Zoo. Elephants and camels were unloaded and then walked up the High Street with their keepers, up West Street, up Whipsnade Road, over the Downs and through the village to the Zoo itself. They caused considerable excitement and people flocked to the

Early January 1932 – animals for the Zoo being walked along High Street North from the Dunstable North station, the photograph taken from our home. The second of the elephants is the famous Dixie, who gave considerable pleasure to the visitors over many years, notably by playing a mouth organ.

streets to see them. They passed right outside our shop and my mother took a photograph of them with her little box Brownie camera, which took hundreds of our snaps without any trouble whatsoever. It was a moment of total fascination and they must have made an extraordinary sight, too, from the lower slopes of the Downs or from the roads below, to see these elephants and camels (actually they were dromedaries) plodding along the top of the Downs, silhouetted against the skyline.

Once it was open I must have gone to the Zoo five or six times a year, it was that interesting for all of us. The Zoo was an outing day, a treat day, a day to be looked forward to. Sometimes, on a Thursday afternoon, the early closing day in Dunstable, in good weather I would walk up with my parents to the bottom of West Street and catch a bus there. On another day my mother and I might catch the mid-morning bus that came through from Bedford and which stopped outside Charlie Smy's shop. However, it would never be certain that we would be able to get on this one, as it could be full of families all going to the Zoo and we therefore preferred to catch a bus from Luton, provided we got there early enough to be near the head of the queue. Such was the popularity of the Zoo, and it seems almost unbelievable to me, now, looking back, that on a hot Sunday in summer or on a bank holiday, the queue of cars returning home late afternoon would stretch literally from the Zoo gates to the crossroads in the centre of Dunstable. But it was so.

The attraction of the Zoo was also heightened in the early days by some of the happenings. In spite of all precautions there was one Himalayan bear that escaped from its paddock a number of times, once roaming over the Downs, early in the morning. There was a fight to the death between two bison – the king of the herd and his challenger – on their hill-side paddock, within close sight of the watching people. It was a reminder of the natural way of life.The fact, too, that wallabies roamed around free, together with peacocks in all their finery, gave spice to a visit. And, of course, there was the large white lion carved out of the hillside and which we looked back on from Ivinghoe Beacon with a certain local pride.

Whether I went to the Zoo with my parents, or with a visiting aunt and uncle or with friends we nearly always took a picnic. There was always an ice-cream to be had, somewhere, too, from one of the kiosks. I never remember eating in the restaurant, there was far too much to see to be indoors, apart from the cost. Picnics were great fun, on the hillside, or sitting on a seat in one of the shelters or near the elephant rides. Before the Zoo had come my parents had picnicked on the open hillside and by the side of Ousely Pond, which for a short time in the early days of Whipsnade Zoo contained alligators.

It was not very long before I had determined the best way round the Zoo. So we nearly always turned right at the entrance and walked along by the shadowy confines of the wood where the wolves were, close by the big bear enclosure and the deer, then out on to the edge of the Zoo to look at the bison and penguins. Then it was along the face of the hillside in an anti-clockwise direction, between the open paddocks and the lions, tigers and polar bears and so on, deviating here and there. Occasionally before starting the round, we would shoot off to have a look at the beavers and take in the flamingoes, both near the restaurant. We reckoned to see every species of animal and bird, more or less, in

It wasn't only children that enjoyed an elephant ride . . . they were very popular, probably more so than the camel and pony rides, but all of them were a feature of the Zoo.
[LZ

the Zoo every time we went, except that we rarely went into the reptile house to look at the snakes, and the shy animals sometimes did not appreciate the importance of coming to see us. There was also a wooded bird sanctuary close by the gates, which I only managed to get into twice because it meant going round with a keeper in a small group, at a definite time and only in certain months of the year. But in there, the guide, by means of holding a small mirror, would be able to show his visitors the nest and eggs inside the nesting box.

I have said that we never had a meal in the restaurant. But occasionally, if we had had a whole day up there and before we caught our bus home we went to a little café for tea and scones, served with small individual jars of jam, at a house outside the Zoo, next to the big car park. It was called 'The House of Pleasant Bread' and the tea-room had been converted from the living accommodation. For a short while, before his family moved away, I knew the boy who lived there. Once he had a birthday party in 'The House of Pleasant Bread' and half-a-dozen of his school friends were invited, when his very courteous, elderly parents looked after us well. They were Quakers, which probably explains on that occasion why the son of the household made more noise than all the rest of us put together.

Whipsnade Zoo, of course, is still very well-known and has enjoyed a tremendous success in breeding, particularly cheetahs. Nowadays I have the pleasure of taking my grand-children there and when I do some of that intense pleasure that I had, in the first decade of the Zoo's existence, still lingers with me. It was a highlight, as a boy living in Dunstable, to go to the Zoo and it still remains so.

Chapter 9

COUNTRY DELIGHT

In the greater part of the time that I am talking about it has to be remembered that Dunstable had no real parks and the only true playing and sitting area in the town was the 'rec' – Bennett's Recreation Ground off Bull Pond Lane. Even that had to be avoided until you were big enough to look after yourself, there were some pretty rough types around. I well remember being in there, against orders, and being 'scragged', my beautiful red and cream coloured Platignum fountain pen being chucked over the fence, never to be seen again. I got no sympathy from home. So for those with very small gardens or none at all, particularly, the countryside just outside the town was important.

I came to love it in any case. There was no shortage of it and I'm satisfied, looking back, that I made the most of it. The simple pleasures of being in the country. Walking, sitting, watching, exploring, playing, picnicking, learning, understanding, appreciating, enjoying just being there.

Our nearest short cut to fields and open country was up Clifton Road, turn right along the extremity of Victoria Street for fifty yards, cross over Chiltern Road and there it was, through a little iron swing gate into the first big meadow. That meadow led in turn, over a stile, to the next one, which came out in Brewers Hill, just near the old 'mill'. Then we had a decision to make – we could either keep going across or we could turn left up the wide lane to where it met the Green Lanes proper.

Sometimes, instead of the Clifton Road way, we would walk up Union Street, cross the unmade Chiltern Road and there were the open fields again. This was before Worthington Road and the Hambling estate was built. Even when they came, in the early thirties, there was an opening at the top of Worthington Road and we could walk into Buttercup Meadow, a very big field that stretched up to meet the trees of the Green Lanes, south to meet West Street and north to join the other fields at the Victoria Street end. All enticing fields and meadows

The Green Lanes, around 1930, stretching away in the direction of Sewell and Totternhoe, the line of the big trees on the right. This picture taken at the junction of the old Brewers Hill lane coming in from the right and, left, the first two lanes that wind down to meet Lancot Hill, the road linking Dunstable and Totternhoe. [OR

to play in and run in and lead us on.

Green Lanes, the ancient British track that was really a drover's way, was a favourite place. (This, of course, was before the great scar of the quarry came and the lane further on had to be deviated round it. Incidentally this desecration led to the formation of The South Beds. Preservation Society). It was always difficult, at first, when you came to the Green Lanes, to decide whether to go in the tall, whispering trees where violets bloomed in early spring, dodging in and out along the little, winding path, playing hide-and-seek, or to walk along the wide open stretch of the lane itself. But at the end of the trees came the start of a low hedge and scrub, at the back of which was a big field where lapwings used to wheel and pierce the air with their strident and plaintive 'Pee-wit' call. Further along, the lane narrowed a little, the hedgerows thickened and became taller and it took on a new perspective. Then, on the left, the dell was reached.

The dell was a landmark place – "Let's go as far as the dell". It was also an action place. We didn't walk past on the chalk-rutted path beside it, we had to go in the dell, down the bank, along the bottom and up the other side. There were a few bushes on the slopes, there were slopes within slopes and it was just a little bit of a mysterious place in that it did not conform to the rest of the Green Lanes. Had something happened there once? Was there a secret? Were we alone?

After that we could carry straight on, right to where the lanes reached Totternhoe Knolls, with its old grass earthworks and ramparts that once were part of a Norman motte and bailey and its confusion of wild flowers, or we could cut across to Sewell, which we mostly did. Down to the lime works, up beside the railway track and the little bridge, along to the Bronze Age camp of Maiden Bower and then back across other field paths until we met Brewers Hill, then home.

With open views across to the line of the Downs and all sorts of interesting things to see it was always a delightful morning or after-noon's pleasure. We deviated all over the place, of course, so that by the time we got home we were often tired out. It was a good area for bird's nesting, too. Blackbird and thrush and hedge-sparrow and linnet in the hedgerows, whitethroat and yellow hammer in the low thickets and scrub, skylark in the grasses of the meadow, corn bunting and meadow pipit.

It was along the Green Lanes and round this area that, when I was at the Grammar School, the cross country races were held, which were completely separate from Sports Day. They both started a hundred yards or so in from the West Street end of the lanes. The Junior race cut across before the dell was reached and came back over the meadows and stiles to the Victoria Street corner, then along Chiltern Road, down the home stretch of West Parade and into the finish in the school playing field, by the pavilion. The Senior race was much longer and went right down to Sewell and round before following the same way back. I was happy to participate, I was expected to do my best for the House, in any case, but I never really enjoyed those cross-countries, not like the other sports. I was not a long-distance runner (a 22-yard sprint was my speciality) and it was a long trek under those circumstances. However, they were bliss compared with the annual Steeplechase.

That took place at Sewell, in the Easter term, and the conditions were always wet and muddy. The race started from a field below one of the farms, by 'kind' permission of the farmer, where we had to change in a big barn. The course was over damp meadows and brooks in a wild area known as 'The Litany', below the hamlet of Sewell. It was generally a case, very shortly after the start, of squelching along. Gates had to be gone through where the ground had been churned up by cows, brooks had to be negotiated by jumping over them (if you were lucky) or crawling up the slippery banks, hedges to be got through. All the time the ground that was being trodden on had to be watched carefully. Cow pats abounded, low thistles were a danger, puddles were everywhere.

The race over, shoes somehow had to be prised off (if not already lost), filthy shirt and shorts taken off, cold water splashed around from a

Although this is a 1950 photograph of the Grammar School steeplechase below Sewell, little had changed! Without doubt, the general idea can be seen. . . .   [DG(GG)

large round wooden tub outside the barn and outer clothes then put back on amongst the hay and straw in the barn. It was, of course, absolute child's play compared with the assault courses that so many of those runners were to undergo in the not-too-distant future. But that was not known and in its way, the steeplechase was a challenge, something to be got through and achieved. Perhaps it played its part in the years that were to come. However, the changing facilities were anything but hygienic and it was little wonder that one year I picked up something that gave me ringworm on my back, and being infectious, caused me to be away from school for a while.

We always used to refer to Sewell, in the family, as Sewell Only. This was because the sign post at the corner of the little road that led off the northern end of the Chalk Cutting said SEWELL ONLY. So Sewell Only it became. But Sewell was a delightful spot and it was always enjoyable to go there. Two farms, a couple of very attractive-looking cottages below the road and a half-dozen or so houses, tucked away from the busy Watling Street. Walking along the road to the railway bridge was always interesting. There would be primroses and white violets in the hedge-side and cowslips on the slopes. The cuckoo could

The annual steeplechase at Sewell – The Start and The Finish. Taken probably in 1937 it can be seen what I mean about the washing and changing facilities! All good stuff. . . . [DGS(1)
[DGS(1)

The Chalk Cutting and beyond, around 1931, the old-style, familiar telegraph poles much in evidence. The path over the top wasn't as precarious as it looks. [LM

often be heard from there. Swallows and martins played round the barns.

One way to Sewell, which we sometimes took, was to go down High Street North and walk over the right-hand side of the Chalk Cutting. This was a super walk, high up over the road, following the little path by the hedge. Sometimes we sat down towards the end, on the top slope of a dell that was there, watching the traffic and looking out over the flat countryside. Then, continuing, the path went down and along the side of a cottage where we were literally going past an upstairs window, as the house was cut into the chalk, part of the tiny community down there, called Chalk Hill, which once upon a time had had its own little chapel. Sewell was then reached by crossing the road, very carefully indeed. (There was also a walk, by turning right at Chalk Hill, that went along the end of the sewage works and came out at Houghton Regis, but that walk did smell a bit. I used to do it every now and again, but no-one else seemed terribly keen).

The Green Lanes, Sewell, Totternhoe Knolls were one area. Another was Well Head, at the end of Tring Road going west, on the right and opposite the entrance to the Gliding Club. I had a friend who lived at the top of Totternhoe Road and as Well Head was close we quite often went down there, particularly when it was tadpole time.

The little stream (the Ouzel) that came out of the bank and mean-

A pencil drawing by Ian Strang, done in 1948. But little has changed from ten to fifteen years earlier. [ML

dered its way down to Doolittle Mill gave Well Head its fascination. Just to be there was fun. There was water to start off with and there was no other water to play in or be near in Dunstable or the immediate outskirts. It was also a stream in a valley, with a deep bank that sloped down from a wide cart track that went along to the mill and to the farm. That added more enjoyment to the scene. So we paddled in the stream and played along the edges and jumped across to The Island, a small area which had become isolated by the brook deviating to two streams. On the island, which was not easy to negotiate because of big clumps of grass and sedges and small bushes, there were kingcups, great big clumps of them and water forget-me-nots. Moorhens scuttled away, red bibs bobbing. Nearer the mill, the stream became wider until it went into forbidden territory round the back of the mill and became the mill race.

Doolittle Mill was a landmark to us, it had a certain fascination. But only once did I go inside and that was because for a while I was friendly with the boy who lived there. He lived with his three elderly great-aunts and he was a bit of a loner, so nobody really went down there, as far as I know. But on this occasion he had a birthday party tea and I was invited. I regret very much, now, that I can't remember much about the inside of the house at Doolittle Mill. Perhaps it was natural, as it was in the summer and we played outside. But I do remember that we had strawberries – real strawberries, a rare luxury for me – for tea, on a big table with lots of old china. There were old pictures on the walls and old chairs, and there wasn't a lot of light in the room, the sun just filtering through small windows. Where we first went in there was a stone floor of quarry tiles.

The outstanding memory etched in my mind, however, was of the three ladies. They were all dressed in Edwardian or Victorian clothes. Their long dresses reached from the floor right up to their necks, were buttoned up to a collar and were trimmed with lace. One of them had a lavender dress. They welcomed us, made sure we had something nice to eat and drink and looked after us. Then they came to the door after tea to wave us goodbye – the ladies of Doolittle Mill.

Well Head was also the place where I had my high spot (well, it was to me) in my world of catching butterflies. This last needs a little explanation, but bear with me.

My father was a keen entomologist, in fact he was a very knowledgable one and gave talks and lectures around Dunstable. He and his twin brother had spent hours and hours, with their butterfly nets, as youths, out in the woods and lanes nearest to their home, often walking miles to get there. Sometimes they went out at night, putting treacle on the trees, then going to see what they had caught the next morning. Father built up a considerable collection of butterflies and moths, mounting them carefully in special cases and clearly identifying them, with any variations, in neat handwriting. The two boys saved up for a long time to purchase Edward Newman's 'The Natural History of British Butterflies & Moths' the standard work of the day. The collection, kept in a special cabinet, was compiled in his younger days, he never added to it or wanted to do so, after he came to Dunstable.

He used to call butterflies 'Living Pictures' and he passed on that enthusiasm and love for them to me. Soon I was looking for the first Brimstone of the year, knew the different ones that came regularly to the buddleia and the ones that drifted into the garden from the fields and hillsides. The lovely little Orange-tip butterfly, white with the bright orange corner to each wing, was a favourite from the very start and the first sight of it each year is still linked in my mind with the first day of summer. Caterpillars were observed and looked up. We had a lot of the hairy, woolly caterpillars of the tiger moth, but it was the sudden sighting one evening of a particular hawk moth caterpillar that caused the greatest excitement.

Hawk moth caterpillars, of which there are a number of varieties, have a horn sticking up at the end. They are also quite large compared with other caterpillars. We had seen the eyed hawk and the lime hawk, but this one was altogether different. It was in fact the caterpillar of the elephant hawk moth. So we picked it up, put it in a box with air holes in the lid and added vegetation for food. Then we found a second one, then a third. Where they had come from we never knew and we never saw one again.

This was late summer. My father made a special box, some two feet square, with gauze all round it and a little door through which food could be placed. The caterpillars, two green and one brown, seemed happy enough, so all was well. In the fullness of time, they each spun their chrysalis and in the fullness of time after that, the following May, three beautiful, velvet-like brown and red moths emerged.

This, of course, was marvellous education, as well as enjoyment, so a butterfly net had to follow, which my father made. I swept it round the garden, picking off whites and tortoiseshells and peacocks and such, then letting them go. On bank holiday picnics I would take it to Ivinghoe Beacon and Ashridge and in early days I used it elsewhere as well. But when I was out in the country with friends, later on, I was inclined to leave it at home. For one reason it tended to get in the way, I didn't always want it anyway, and secondly I was aware that one or two of my pals thought it a bit odd to have a friend who was waving a butterfly net around. They were probably quite right.

But on this occasion at Well Head (yes, we are back again) I had the net with me when a Clouded Yellow suddenly flew past, along the wide cartway at the top. I had never seen one before, but I instinctively knew what it was and I gave chase. By luck more than judgement I managed to catch it, some hundred yards on and transfer it to one of the special little round boxes that I had with me. I was as pleased as the proverbial Punch, absolutely thrilled – a Clouded Yellow – not a rare butterfly, but not all that common either and to catch one, let alone see one . . . phew! What would Dad say?

I had hardly started retracing my footsteps when lo and behold, sunning itself on the dry cart track, was a Painted Lady (I am still talking about butterflies, by the way). A quick swoosh and that one went into another box. Another real find, another real catch! I could hardly wait to get home. My father, of course, was delighted and gave me a shilling out of the till. Then I went out into the garden, gazed at them for about half-an-hour and let them fly away.

So Well Head had its memories. But another walk was along the southern stretch of Bull Pond Lane, when it really was a lane. Just a couple of houses on one corner and a bungalow, standing back, half way along. Otherwise farm fields. Opposite the top of Garden Road stood

the old-established engineering works of Harrison Carter, next to that a
farmhouse. (Harrison Carter closed soon after the last war, but a large
advertisement for this firm can still be seen painted on the side of a
house at the bottom of Garden Road. It was also very close to these
works that, in the First World War, a Zeppelin, being chased by a
fighter plane, dropped a small bomb, thereby leaving a small crater in
the field). Where Bull Pond Lane met Periwinkle Lane (was there, I
used to wonder, once upon a time, a lane bordered by the mauve
periwinkle flowers? Answer: Yes, banks covered in them) the first
meadow started, which led eventually over the fields to Kensworth. This
was an interesting ramble, across an ancient British track, alongside
thick hedgerows, past fields of waving corn in summer and out at the
back of Kensworth Church. Alternatively, up Isle of Wight Lane to
meet the little road that comes off the top of the Downs at Robertson's
Corner and journeys on to the village of Kensworth.

The pleasant thing about this ramble, too, was that it could be done
with several variations, so that it was not out and back the same way.
One of these was a path up the side of Half-Moon Dairy (now Mr.
Hughes, the furniture maker) at the end of the town off High Street
South (the stretch known as Half Moon Hill), and along the back of the
big water tower, beyond which the way could be joined again. It was
instant green fields as soon as the path off the main road was turned
into.

Another route was across the fields on which First Avenue now stands
and over the hill which is now part of the Laing estate. This led to the
spinney of tall trees and the scrub at the side of the golf course and
skirting this the paths led over pastures where the huge quarry has now
eaten into the countryside. In Spring you could literally walk on
cowslips, there. Hundreds and hundreds of them. Now they have to be
looked for. Now the old way to Kensworth is no longer and roads have
to be walked along, not nearly so inviting.

I look back on all these rambles and walks and explorations and the
places where we ran and played with the greatest of pleasure. I have a
particular affection for all the meadows and fields that linked with the
Green Lanes and Sewell because I suppose so many of them are no
longer there, swallowed up in the expansion of the town. Also because
that area was the closest to home and one that I automatically tended
towards in early years.

But there is one place, one area, that I haven't mentioned yet and
which I have left to the last because for me it means something more
than any other piece of countryside. The Downs – Dunstable Downs –
John Bunyan's 'Delectable Mountains'.

Chapter 10

THE DOWNS

'God gives all men all earth to love,
But since man's heart is small,
Ordains for each one spot shall prove
Beloved over all.
Each to his choice . . .'

My first recollections of Dunstable Downs are twofold. One is in winter, one in summer.

The summer one is being up there one afternoon with my mother and running up and down the little chalk path that had been worn over the top of the Five Knolls. Up the slope, over the top, down the slope and on again. Up and down, up and down.

The winter memory is of sitting on a sledge, warmly wrapped up on the very lower slopes with thick snow on the ground. It was after dark, but there was a clear sky and the glare of the snow lit up everything. Then being pulled home along West Street itself, on the road, by my sister and the two Pickering girls. There was no traffic and it was all very still, as I was pulled along by the side of the hedges and meadows that bordered West Street, to the corner of Chiltern Road, where the clanking, hissing Primrose laundry used to stand, and down.

Sledging, of course (tobogganing was not the word we used, it was always sledging: "Are you coming sledging?" we would say) was very much part of the boyhood scene and it seems to me now, looking back, that we went sledging every winter because it always snowed every winter, sometimes for a long spell. When the snow was just right the lower slopes of the Downs were perfect for it and by starting at the top, just below the Knolls, we whizzed down towards West Street. It was tremendous enjoyment and if a really good run was had it was possible to carry on across the road and down the bank on the other side to finish near Mr. Rollings' whiting sheds. There were two things that had to be avoided – the dell, on the left, soon after starting, and the hedge. If you

*An early sledging expedition.
With my sister (centre) and
Ella and Elizabeth Pickering.*

caught the edge of the dell you were likely to end up at the bottom of it with the sledge following fast. Whipsnade Road on the other side was no problem and unless anyone was wildly off course there was no fear of tumbling across that road and ending up near the Rifle Volunteer public house that stood at the corner of that road and West Street.

Snow, of course, was always magical to us boys and over the top of the Downs we went in winter, just as we did in all seasons. Snowdrifts had to be gone into and out of with our wellington boots on, the way down the bigger slopes to the path at the bottom had to be negotiated in a different manner, tumbles were taken, snowball fights took place. There was excitement being on top of the Downs when the snow lay thick and a whole carpet of dazzling white stretched out and away over the vale, as far as the eye could see.

Dunstablians used the Downs, nearly 800 ft. above sea level, very much as their 'park', only this park had a magnificent view. It meant a lot to them and in those days of quiet pleasures those who were minded so to do would come out on a summer evening or at weekends, just to walk and sit and look. There were wooden seats along the top then, above and around Pascombe Pit. Just a simple, thick wooden bench on two stout supports. Thousands of people had sat on them. In so doing their feet had worn away all the grass and in front of each one and at the ends there was a bowl of chalk. Initials were carved on them, too. As boys we didn't really sit on the benches, we were far too active for that, but there was also a timber look-out post, some ten feet high, with iron rings in it and that would never be passed without climbing up it. On a windy day, with breath almost taken away by the gale, it was even

1st March, 1931. A view, from just below the Knolls, looking down the slope and across a more or less unsullied Dunstable, toward Houghton Regis. 'The Rifle Volunteer' is the nearest building, the line of the Green Lanes just starting opposite, by the trees. A very indistinct West Street divides them. [OR

The sign of 'The Rifle Volunteer', demolished in 1969. At the turn of the century it was advertised as a good place to come to for the 'bracing air' of Dunstable Downs. [LM

A scene similar to the winter photograph, but in summer and some fifteen months later, in 1932. Across from 'The Rifle Volunteer', a prominently advertised café that was there for a few years. Beyond that the beginnings of the Hambling Estate with Franklin Road joining Worthington Road running toward, but not reaching Green Lanes. But the meadows are still there, off West Street and stretching away. In the centre distance the cement works at Houghton Regis, with its tall chimney. In front of the works, almost lost, the chimney of Bennett's Brewery. To the right the next chimney is that of Waterlow's and on the edge of the picture, Bagshawe's foundry chimney, which belched forth tongues of fire each evening, when the foundry was being shut down. On the left of the photograph, behind the hedge, the Downs Garage and by the thick trees of Green Lanes, the sheds of Mr. Rollings' whiting works. Over the Green Lanes, in the distance, are the round cylinders of the Gas Works. [OR

144

windier up there and even more breathless. But the post had to be climbed, so we climbed it.

Our rambles over the Downs would mainly be up the gradual slope from West Street, skirt Pascombe Pit, along the top until the bushes became more abundant, down the slope and along the bottom path all the way to the lower slopes again, walking along the back of the long gardens of the houses in Tring Road. It was nearly always in that direction, as then the steep slope didn't have to be climbed, but again there were many deviations. We hardly ever climbed down or up Pascombe Pit itself and rarely went the whole way to Whipsnade.

Along the top there were the old bunkers, now grassed over, of the Golf Club when there were holes on the Downs side of the road. At the foot there were barrows that once had been opened, as well as the Five Knolls on top. There was the drum that winched the gliders up and where we would hang on to the wing tips at the direction of the pilot as the glider bumped its way down in an effort (mostly in vain) to become airborne. There were the gliders themselves to watch. There were the bushes on the slopes near the Gliding Club field that harboured wild life. There were the little winding paths along the face of the slopes, often half hidden amongst the grasses. There were so many places to play around, to explore, to look for different things. It was a boy's paradise.

Spring and summer were the loveliest times to be up on the Downs. There were the downland wild flowers, some clearly seen, some to be looked for in hidden places. Cowslips, early purple orchids, pink rest-harrow with its spiny stems, the lovely deep purple bellflower, lady's slipper, scabious in profusion, thistles. We used to snap off the dried heads of knapweed and throw them at the person in front. Retaliation resulted.

Bird's-nesting was a favourite pastime, but I'm glad to say that we were never terribly successful. Blackbirds and thrushes didn't really interest us, they were common place, a magpie's nest was exceedingly difficult to get to with its dome and at the top of a prickly hawthorn and it was just as well we didn't really try that much, whilst we never had enough patience to sit and watch and wait and watch again for any ground-nesting bird, to discover its nest – we were far too easy to fool.

The skylark was the bird of the Downs in those days. Now they are scarce where once they were in profusion. The song of a skylark – the blithe spirit of the poet – on a sunlit spring or summer morning, up there on the Downs, will ever remain in the memory, as it must do to thousands of other people. To listen to those ascending, joyful notes as this tiny bird soars ever upwards, hovers and falls again in slow movements before it suddenly darts to earth, never ceases to remind me, wherever I might be, of those skylarks that sang over the Downs.

Only once did I find a skylark's nest in that vicinity, in spite of their number and that was because we had a family picnic some thirty or forty yards away from one and I was in a position, when I saw the first descent, to just watch very carefully until I had the spot pinpointed. Then to look down on that cluster of five mottled brown eggs, carefully tucked away in a grass cup, was to add to the happiness of listening to the song.

If the skylark was the bird to be remembered (not forgetting the twittering of linnets and in winter small flocks of long-tailed tits), then the insect that captivated us was the burnet moth. Along with the downland flowers, so there were the butterflies of the chalk hills and surrounding fields – small heath, meadow brown, ringlet, wall, speckled wood, grayling, small skipper, the blues including the chalk-hill blue, small copper, marbled white, orange-tip, tortoiseshell, peacock, the whites, sometimes a dark green fritillery. But the burnet moth was something different.

To start off with it is a day-flying moth, not a butterfly. Then it is a lovely little moth with near black front wings and crimson hind wings; on each of the top wings are five or six (according to the species) bright red spots. Thirdly it flies in high summer and only when it is dry and warm, so to see them hover and buzz around means a lovely day. Fourthly – and this is the telling point – they emerge from tiny little yellow-coloured cocoons hung high on grass stems and old flower stalks.

In the right place on the downland slopes there would be lots of these cocoons. I used to pick a dozen or so, take them home and put them in a jam jar on a window sill in the sun. This was not fully appreciated by my mother, who was not taken with the idea of cocoons in her clean house, out of which would come stray moths. However they stayed and, sure enough, one morning there would be a buzzing from inside one of the cocoons and a dark object would be seen outlined. Soon the thin cover would be broken, a brand new burnet moth would emerge and cling to the stalk. That was the time to take the jar out into the garden and let that one fly away, not before, I would add, it was determined whether it was a five-spot or a six-spot burnet.

There was always a feeling, on the Downs, of ancient history, particularly perhaps when the mist drifted along the vale or in winter, when the slopes were less green or where they were bare-backed. Of course it *was* a place of history and I had been told of the ancient Britons roaming the hills, looking for food, and of a gibbet that once had stood on the Downs where anyone found stealing a sheep was hanged. There were true stories of skeletons being found and odd bones and flints and fossils and bits of pottery and crude tools of some long-forgotten tribe. After all, the Five Knolls were really round barrows constructed by these local tribes over 4,000 years ago to bury their dead at the time of the late Neolithic or early Bronze age. They were known burial grounds, but there were all sorts of bumps and hillocks and dips in the ground that conjured up the imagination. 'Local Schoolboy Makes Historic Find on Dunstable Downs' was a newspaper heading that was a day-time dream.

It was natural, living in Dunstable on the road where the Roman legions had marched and where, later, highwaymen rode their big, black horses to rob travellers at pistol point, to imbibe all this history and to know, as well as feel, that the Downs were part of it. This was also reflected when I looked back to the line of the Downs and to the steep bare slopes of Pascombe Pit from Well Head or from one of the small roads running out of Totternhoe or Eaton Bray. I could imagine . . . and duly did!

But it was the superb view from the Downs that really made them so captivating. On a clear day some sixty miles, way out to the Cotswolds, to distant hills, over meadows and fields and villages, across the plain of England. Ivinghoe Beacon, close by, where an Armada beacon was lit over 400 years ago in that warning chain that spread through the length and breadth of the country and where it is rumoured Queen Boadicea (Boudicca) is buried; the churches – the elegant, tall spire of Leighton Buzzard's All Saints, the 13th century one of St. Giles, patron saint of cripples, at Totternhoe, looking very much a typical country village church, half-hidden in a cluster of green trees, the dominant one at Edlesborough, perched on the hill to which the villagers had moved it in one night, hearing that the Devil was coming to sack the original site, thus thwarting the Devil, the comforting, solid outline of another All Saints, at Tilsworth, nestling in the slopes of the meadows behind; the line of tall trees in Green Lanes, leading to the thick slopes of Totternhoe Knolls and the grass ramparts of the 'castle'; the sun glinting and reflecting on Mr. Wallace's glass houses in Eaton Bray, where thousands of carnations were grown and from where they were packed to be sent not only throughout Great Britain but all over the world – the first pick-up of their journey was made by the little train, (the 'Skimpot Flyer') stopping at Stanbridgeford station; Doolittle Mill and Bellows Mill; farms and farmhouses; gardens; hedges and spinneys; lanes and winding roads, out, out and beyond. On a clear day, magnificent. On a hazy day, early in the morning with the promise of hot sun to come, another kind of quality, felt as well as seen. At the end of the day, with the sun setting in a blaze of colours, majesty also.

Of course the view is still there and, thank goodness, it is very largely unspoilt. The villages have sprawled out a little, Leighton Buzzard is bigger, the greenhouses and the carnations, alas, have gone, the line of Green Lanes has been altered, Indians sometimes send out smoke signals from behind the Beacon, there is no puff-puff from the little train. But if you can avoid seeing the television aerials of the nearby houses, the view is almost the same.

If I was the other side of the world I could shut my eyes a thousand times and still see the view as it is to-day and as I knew it fifty to sixty years ago. I did not realise it, of course, as a boy, but it was those boyhood days, on the gentle hills above the market town, that gave me that special feeling of the Downs, one that still exists. I did not know then, in my almost non-existent travels outside Bedfordshire and the borders of Hertfordshire and Buckinghamshire, that I would see so much of the world, thereby giving me a different outlook and concep- tion of life.

However, through RNVR days on behalf of His Majesty and then because of the company for which I worked, plus a few holiday breaks here and there, I have been fortunate to at least see a part of many countries and can make comparisons therefore.

So I have looked down on Greenland's icy mountains and trodden India's coral strand; travelled through the green pastures of New Zealand and the plantations of Ceylon (as it was then); stood on the banks of the Tigris and the Jordan and the Danube and the Nile and the Seine and the Yarra and the Vistula and the Tiber (what did the verse say about Horatius in my Junior School Poetry that I was told to learn by heart? – 'O Tiber! father Tiber! To whom the Romans pray, A Roman's life, a Roman's arms, Take thou in charge this day!'); flown over the Ganges and the Mississippi, the Alps and the Andes; gazed at the splendour of Sydney Harbour and watched the never-ending water traffic of the Bosporus and the Golden Horn; stood with feet astride over two tiny streams at the Great Divide, one of which eventually flows into the Atlantic and one into the Pacific; walked along the pink beaches of Bermuda and the white sands of Antigua and Tobago (where I spent a Sunday afternoon reading that most English of books – 'Watership Down'); looked in awe at Gulfoss – 'The Golden Waterfall' – in Iceland and Victoria Falls – 'The Smoke that Thunders'; drunk in the sheer magical scene of Rarotonga, in the Cook Islands, with its translucent water and coral reefs and the vivid colour of flamboyants, bougainvil- laea and hibiscus; strolled under the delicate mauve jacaranda and the bright flame lily and tulip trees of an African city; gazed across to the peaks of the Rockies and the mountains outside Teheran; taken in the history of Lebanon, that once-lovely and fascinating country, of the Holy Land, of Ethiopia; picnicked among the gum trees and wattle of Australia, with kookaburras calling; seen from the summit tops, the wide sweep of the bay at Rio de Janeiro, the coastline of Vancouver, the hubbub of Hong Kong. Cities, towns, countries, islands, all with their charm, all with their own particular quality.

But . . . but . . . and including so much seen in England which I would never want to leave – the view from Glastonbury Tor, that stretch of North Cornish coast that we know so well, that Sussex village, that Yorkshire dale, those bluebell woods in Dorset, that winding, tree-girt river in Devon and so many more – none can quite compare, for me, with the view from the Downs. This is my native heath, nurtured from boyhood, strengthened in manhood because of those days and transcending anything else. I still get a tingle down the spine, sometimes, as I walk the paths and look out across the shires of England.

'God gives all men all earth to love' – yes. And in this small stretch of downland and continuing Rudyard Kipling's words, but with a different scene, then it is with these Downs that 'I rejoice, the lot has fallen to me. . .'

[DTC

149

RETROSPECTION

Dunstable wasn't slow in holding big fêtes and special days for some cause or another, there was a keen community sense. The proposed new Luton & Dunstable Hospital, to be built in the thirties, was a good example and many events took place to raise money towards that aim. This photograph shows such an event – Hospital Sunday parade in late September 1931, taken from the balcony of the Town Hall. The narrow entrance to Church Street can be seen clearly, with the sign of the Red Lion Hotel hanging out proudly on one corner and the Home & Colonial grocery stores on the other. The Westminster Bank, next to the hotel, shows its former facade. The cross-roads sign post has a new arm added to it – TO THE ZOO. An Eastern National bus comes to a halt as the procession, headed by the Grammar School Cadet Corps Band, makes its way through the centre of the town. On a sunlit, mild day, the citizens of Dunstable come out in their hundreds to enjoy the spectacle.   [JD

KEY TO PHOTOGRAPHS

BB	Miss Betty Brookes
BP	Dr. Brian Parsons
CDM	Carr & Day & Martin Ltd.
CS	Miss Christina Scott
DD	Official Guide to Dunstable and District, Index Publishers, 1933
DG	Dunstable Gazette
DG (EB)	Dunstable Gazette, original lent by Mrs. Elizabeth Bilk
DG (GG)	Dunstable Gazette, George Gurney collection
DGS (1)	Dunstable Grammar School 50th Anniversary Souvenir booklet
DGS (2)	Dunstable Grammar School Magazine, Summer Term, 1938
DS	David Sewell
DTC	Dunstable Town Council
FTM	Fred Moore
GH	Borough of Dunstable booklet – Official Opening, Grove House Pleasure Grounds, lent by Miss Elsie England
JD	John Dandy
JT	James Tibbett's Dunstable Guide, 1923
LM	Luton Museum
LZ	Zoological Society of London
MC	Methodist Church, The Square
ML	Mrs. Muriel Linney
OR	Omer Roucoux collection
PC (DS)	Post-card lent by David Sewell
RB	Roger Barton
SB	Mrs. Sydney Bird
SJ	Borough of Dunstable, Silver Jubilee Celebrations, Official Programme, lent by Mrs. Joyce Cook
WZ	'The Whipsnade Zoo' (W. S. Berridge) – frontispiece

Books Published by
THE BOOK CASTLE

NORTH CHILTERNS CAMERA, 1863–1954; FROM THE THURSTON COLLECTION IN LUTON MUSEUM: edited by Stephen Bunker
Rural landscapes, town views, studio pictures and unique royal portraits by the area's leading early photographer.

JOURNEYS INTO BEDFORDSHIRE: Anthony Mackay
Foreword by The Marquess of Tavistock
A lavish book of over 150 evocative ink drawings.

FOLK: CHARACTERS and EVENTS in the HISTORY OF BEDFORDSHIRE and NORTHAMPTONSHIRE: Vivienne Evans
Arranged by village/town, an anthology of stories about the counties' most intriguing historical figures.

ECHOES: TALES and LEGENDS of BEDFORDSHIRE and HERTFORDSHIRE: Vic Lea
Thirty, compulsively retold historical incidents.

TERESA of WATLING STREET: Arnold Bennett
Introduced by Simon Houfe
The only detective story by one of the twentieth century's most famous novelists. Written and set in Bedfordshire.

A LASTING IMPRESSION: Michael Dundrow
An East End boy's wartime experiences as an evacuee on a Chilterns farm at Totternhoe.

JOHN BUNYAN: HIS LIFE and TIMES: Vivienne Evans
Foreword by the Bishop of Bedford
Bedfordshire's most famous son set in his seventeenth century context.

LOCAL WALKS: SOUTH BEDFORDSHIRE and NORTH CHILTERNS: Vaughan Basham
Twenty seven thematic circular walks.

DUNSTABLE DECADE: THE EIGHTIES – A collection of photographs: Pat Lovering
A souvenir book of nearly 300 pictures of people and events in the 1980s.

DUNSTABLE IN DETAIL: Nigel Benson
A hundred of the town's buildings and features, past and present, plus town-trail map.

OLD DUNSTABLE: Bill Twaddle
A new edition of this collection of early photographs.

ROYAL HOUGHTON: Pat Lovering
Illustrated history of Houghton Regis from earliest times to the present day.

OLD HOUGHTON, INCLUDING UPPER HOUGHTON, NOW PART OF DUNSTABLE: Pat Lovering
Over 170 photographs of Houghton Regis during the last 100 years.

Further titles are in preparation.
All the above are available via any bookshop,
or from the publisher and bookseller
THE BOOK CASTLE
12 Church Street, Dunstable, Bedfordshire LU5 4RU. Tel (0582) 605670